Table Of Contents

Table Of Contents

Name: —————————— Date: ——————

Comparing Fractions

Time:

:

Score:

/100

Compare the fractions.   2 points per question

1) $\frac{3}{8}$ $\frac{1}{4}$ 2) $\frac{5}{9}$ $\frac{2}{3}$ 3) $\frac{3}{6}$ $\frac{3}{5}$ 4) $\frac{8}{9}$ $\frac{2}{8}$

5) $\frac{3}{4}$ $\frac{3}{6}$ 6) $\frac{2}{5}$ $\frac{2}{3}$ 7) $\frac{2}{6}$ $\frac{3}{9}$ 8) $\frac{4}{5}$ $\frac{2}{8}$

9) $\frac{2}{4}$ $\frac{2}{3}$ 10) $\frac{2}{4}$ $\frac{6}{8}$ 11) $\frac{2}{3}$ $\frac{1}{5}$ 12) $\frac{1}{9}$ $\frac{1}{6}$

13) $\frac{3}{4}$ $\frac{1}{6}$ 14) $\frac{3}{5}$ $\frac{6}{9}$ 15) $\frac{4}{8}$ $\frac{2}{3}$ 16) $\frac{2}{4}$ $\frac{2}{6}$

17) $\frac{3}{9}$ $\frac{7}{8}$ 18) $\frac{1}{3}$ $\frac{4}{5}$ 19) $\frac{3}{5}$ $\frac{2}{4}$ 20) $\frac{6}{8}$ $\frac{1}{9}$

Compare the fractions.

1) $\frac{2}{8}$ $\frac{2}{7}$ 2) $\frac{2}{5}$ $\frac{1}{4}$ 3) $\frac{1}{7}$ $\frac{2}{10}$ 4) $\frac{7}{8}$ $\frac{4}{6}$

5) $\frac{2}{3}$ $\frac{4}{5}$ 6) $\frac{4}{9}$ $\frac{5}{7}$ 7) $\frac{7}{9}$ $\frac{1}{6}$ 8) $\frac{5}{10}$ $\frac{2}{3}$

9) $\frac{2}{5}$ $\frac{4}{8}$ 10) $\frac{2}{4}$ $\frac{2}{3}$ 11) $\frac{3}{7}$ $\frac{1}{4}$ 12) $\frac{3}{6}$ $\frac{1}{5}$

13) $\frac{8}{10}$ $\frac{3}{8}$ 14) $\frac{4}{9}$ $\frac{6}{10}$ 15) $\frac{2}{5}$ $\frac{7}{8}$ 16) $\frac{2}{4}$ $\frac{2}{9}$

17) $\frac{1}{3}$ $\frac{5}{6}$ 18) $\frac{2}{7}$ $\frac{1}{8}$ 19) $\frac{5}{6}$ $\frac{4}{7}$ 20) $\frac{7}{9}$ $\frac{6}{10}$

21) $\frac{3}{4}$ $\frac{2}{6}$ 22) $\frac{4}{5}$ $\frac{7}{8}$ 23) $\frac{1}{9}$ $\frac{2}{7}$ 24) $\frac{1}{3}$ $\frac{3}{10}$

25) $\frac{1}{4}$ $\frac{2}{3}$ 26) $\frac{6}{10}$ $\frac{3}{9}$ 27) $\frac{5}{7}$ $\frac{1}{8}$ 28) $\frac{3}{5}$ $\frac{2}{6}$

29) $\frac{2}{4}$ $\frac{3}{5}$ 30) $\frac{3}{4}$ $\frac{3}{10}$

Name: ——————————— Date: ——————

Comparing Fractions

Time:
:

Score:
/100

Compare the fractions.   2 points per question

(1) $\frac{6}{8}$ $\frac{3}{5}$ (2) $\frac{3}{4}$ $\frac{1}{3}$ (3) $\frac{4}{6}$ $\frac{3}{8}$ (4) $\frac{5}{6}$ $\frac{1}{3}$

(5) $\frac{3}{4}$ $\frac{4}{5}$ (6) $\frac{5}{8}$ $\frac{2}{6}$ (7) $\frac{1}{5}$ $\frac{2}{4}$ (8) $\frac{2}{3}$ $\frac{4}{5}$

(9) $\frac{1}{3}$ $\frac{1}{4}$ (10) $\frac{2}{8}$ $\frac{2}{6}$ (11) $\frac{2}{3}$ $\frac{4}{8}$ (12) $\frac{1}{4}$ $\frac{1}{5}$

(13) $\frac{3}{6}$ $\frac{7}{8}$ (14) $\frac{3}{5}$ $\frac{2}{3}$ (15) $\frac{1}{4}$ $\frac{5}{6}$ (16) $\frac{5}{6}$ $\frac{3}{5}$

(17) $\frac{2}{4}$ $\frac{4}{8}$ (18) $\frac{1}{3}$ $\frac{2}{8}$ (19) $\frac{4}{5}$ $\frac{3}{6}$ (20) $\frac{3}{4}$ $\frac{2}{3}$

Compare the fractions.

1) $\dfrac{2}{3}$ $\dfrac{2}{7}$ 2) $\dfrac{4}{5}$ $\dfrac{3}{4}$ 3) $\dfrac{2}{6}$ $\dfrac{2}{8}$ 4) $\dfrac{7}{10}$ $\dfrac{1}{3}$

5) $\dfrac{1}{9}$ $\dfrac{3}{4}$ 6) $\dfrac{1}{10}$ $\dfrac{3}{8}$ 7) $\dfrac{4}{7}$ $\dfrac{5}{6}$ 8) $\dfrac{2}{3}$ $\dfrac{6}{9}$

9) $\dfrac{2}{5}$ $\dfrac{3}{9}$ 10) $\dfrac{2}{3}$ $\dfrac{4}{6}$ 11) $\dfrac{2}{8}$ $\dfrac{2}{7}$ 12) $\dfrac{2}{10}$ $\dfrac{2}{4}$

13) $\dfrac{2}{5}$ $\dfrac{2}{5}$ 14) $\dfrac{2}{7}$ $\dfrac{1}{3}$ 15) $\dfrac{4}{8}$ $\dfrac{3}{4}$ 16) $\dfrac{1}{9}$ $\dfrac{6}{10}$

17) $\dfrac{1}{6}$ $\dfrac{3}{4}$ 18) $\dfrac{2}{3}$ $\dfrac{3}{5}$ 19) $\dfrac{1}{6}$ $\dfrac{2}{9}$ 20) $\dfrac{3}{10}$ $\dfrac{4}{8}$

21) $\dfrac{5}{7}$ $\dfrac{3}{4}$ 22) $\dfrac{2}{5}$ $\dfrac{1}{3}$ 23) $\dfrac{3}{6}$ $\dfrac{1}{7}$ 24) $\dfrac{7}{10}$ $\dfrac{8}{9}$

25) $\dfrac{7}{8}$ $\dfrac{1}{3}$ 26) $\dfrac{6}{10}$ $\dfrac{3}{4}$ 27) $\dfrac{2}{7}$ $\dfrac{4}{5}$ 28) $\dfrac{2}{9}$ $\dfrac{4}{8}$

29) $\dfrac{1}{6}$ $\dfrac{1}{3}$ 30) $\dfrac{3}{6}$ $\dfrac{3}{4}$

Name: —————————————— Date: ———————

Simplifying Fractions

Time:
:

Score:
/100

Simplify the fractions.

2 points per question

1) $\frac{21}{28} =$

2) $\frac{4}{8} =$

3) $\frac{7}{21} =$

4) $\frac{18}{54} =$

5) $\frac{27}{45} =$

6) $\frac{32}{80} =$

7) $\frac{6}{12} =$

8) $\frac{2}{20} =$

9) $\frac{6}{18} =$

10) $\frac{56}{72} =$

11) $\frac{27}{72} =$

12) $\frac{3}{12} =$

13) $\frac{25}{30} =$

14) $\frac{3}{15} =$

15) $\frac{40}{64} =$

16) $\frac{14}{21} =$

17) $\frac{5}{10} =$

18) $\frac{2}{12} =$

19) $\frac{6}{20} =$

20) $\frac{18}{36} =$

Simplify the fractions.

(1) $\dfrac{18}{30} =$ (2) $\dfrac{10}{12} =$ (3) $\dfrac{4}{12} =$ (4) $\dfrac{49}{63} =$

(5) $\dfrac{10}{20} =$ (6) $\dfrac{16}{80} =$ (7) $\dfrac{8}{12} =$ (8) $\dfrac{8}{64} =$

(9) $\dfrac{9}{15} =$ (10) $\dfrac{6}{12} =$ (11) $\dfrac{6}{8} =$ (12) $\dfrac{3}{6} =$

(13) $\dfrac{3}{27} =$ (14) $\dfrac{2}{12} =$ (15) $\dfrac{5}{25} =$ (16) $\dfrac{18}{60} =$

(17) $\dfrac{35}{45} =$ (18) $\dfrac{8}{24} =$ (19) $\dfrac{20}{32} =$ (20) $\dfrac{16}{20} =$

(21) $\dfrac{40}{48} =$ (22) $\dfrac{4}{16} =$ (23) $\dfrac{6}{18} =$ (24) $\dfrac{42}{56} =$

(25) $\dfrac{9}{81} =$ (26) $\dfrac{15}{20} =$ (27) $\dfrac{18}{24} =$ (28) $\dfrac{12}{18} =$

(29) $\dfrac{10}{50} =$ (30) $\dfrac{12}{30} =$

Name: _____ Date: _____

Simplifying Fractions

Time:

:

Score:

/100

Simplify the fractions.

2 points per question

① $\dfrac{18}{36}$ =

② $\dfrac{6}{18}$ =

③ $\dfrac{4}{8}$ =

④ $\dfrac{12}{24}$ =

⑤ $\dfrac{15}{25}$ =

⑥ $\dfrac{4}{12}$ =

⑦ $\dfrac{6}{12}$ =

⑧ $\dfrac{4}{16}$ =

⑨ $\dfrac{9}{27}$ =

⑩ $\dfrac{25}{30}$ =

⑪ $\dfrac{30}{40}$ =

⑫ $\dfrac{18}{60}$ =

⑬ $\dfrac{9}{45}$ =

⑭ $\dfrac{28}{40}$ =

⑮ $\dfrac{9}{18}$ =

⑯ $\dfrac{72}{81}$ =

⑰ $\dfrac{15}{30}$ =

⑱ $\dfrac{35}{56}$ =

⑲ $\dfrac{14}{21}$ =

⑳ $\dfrac{8}{64}$ =

Simplify the fractions.

(1) $\frac{10}{30}$ =

(2) $\frac{4}{8}$ =

(3) $\frac{4}{12}$ =

(4) $\frac{3}{18}$ =

(5) $\frac{30}{45}$ =

(6) $\frac{12}{16}$ =

(7) $\frac{81}{90}$ =

(8) $\frac{27}{36}$ =

(9) $\frac{6}{12}$ =

(10) $\frac{16}{20}$ =

(11) $\frac{40}{45}$ =

(12) $\frac{9}{18}$ =

(13) $\frac{30}{40}$ =

(14) $\frac{6}{36}$ =

(15) $\frac{28}{35}$ =

(16) $\frac{9}{30}$ =

(17) $\frac{2}{8}$ =

(18) $\frac{24}{30}$ =

(19) $\frac{20}{50}$ =

(20) $\frac{7}{28}$ =

(21) $\frac{3}{6}$ =

(22) $\frac{30}{54}$ =

(23) $\frac{6}{18}$ =

(24) $\frac{40}{64}$ =

(25) $\frac{12}{24}$ =

(26) $\frac{21}{56}$ =

(27) $\frac{63}{81}$ =

(28) $\frac{8}{16}$ =

(29) $\frac{16}{24}$ =

(30) $\frac{21}{42}$ =

Name: —————————————— Date: ——————

Equivalent Fractions

Time:

:

Score:

/100

Complete the equivalent fractions.

2 points per question

① $\dfrac{}{6} = \dfrac{28}{42}$

② $\dfrac{1}{2} = \dfrac{7}{}$

③ $\dfrac{5}{8} = \dfrac{40}{}$

④ $\dfrac{3}{4} = \dfrac{}{24}$

⑤ $\dfrac{}{3} = \dfrac{14}{21}$

⑥ $\dfrac{5}{9} = \dfrac{}{81}$

⑦ $\dfrac{3}{} = \dfrac{12}{20}$

⑧ $\dfrac{1}{3} = \dfrac{}{12}$

⑨ $\dfrac{4}{} = \dfrac{20}{35}$

⑩ $\dfrac{6}{9} = \dfrac{}{36}$

⑪ $\dfrac{2}{6} = \dfrac{4}{}$

⑫ $\dfrac{1}{} = \dfrac{4}{20}$

⑬ $\dfrac{3}{4} = \dfrac{}{12}$

⑭ $\dfrac{2}{} = \dfrac{16}{64}$

⑮ $\dfrac{1}{2} = \dfrac{}{16}$

⑯ $\dfrac{1}{} = \dfrac{4}{8}$

⑰ $\dfrac{}{4} = \dfrac{2}{8}$

⑱ $\dfrac{5}{} = \dfrac{25}{40}$

⑲ $\dfrac{2}{} = \dfrac{8}{12}$

⑳ $\dfrac{3}{6} = \dfrac{9}{}$

Complete the equivalent fractions.

1. $\dfrac{5}{} = \dfrac{25}{30}$

2. $\dfrac{}{4} = \dfrac{2}{8}$

3. $\dfrac{2}{} = \dfrac{12}{24}$

4. $\dfrac{1}{6} = \dfrac{4}{}$

5. $\dfrac{5}{8} = \dfrac{}{32}$

6. $\dfrac{2}{} = \dfrac{16}{24}$

7. $\dfrac{2}{5} = \dfrac{}{50}$

8. $\dfrac{3}{} = \dfrac{24}{48}$

9. $\dfrac{7}{8} = \dfrac{}{32}$

10. $\dfrac{3}{4} = \dfrac{21}{}$

11. $\dfrac{}{5} = \dfrac{4}{20}$

12. $\dfrac{}{3} = \dfrac{4}{6}$

13. $\dfrac{4}{6} = \dfrac{}{48}$

14. $\dfrac{3}{5} = \dfrac{21}{}$

15. $\dfrac{1}{} = \dfrac{8}{64}$

16. $\dfrac{2}{3} = \dfrac{14}{}$

17. $\dfrac{1}{4} = \dfrac{}{12}$

18. $\dfrac{2}{6} = \dfrac{}{24}$

19. $\dfrac{1}{} = \dfrac{9}{27}$

20. $\dfrac{1}{8} = \dfrac{4}{}$

21. $\dfrac{1}{} = \dfrac{6}{30}$

22. $\dfrac{4}{6} = \dfrac{}{54}$

23. $\dfrac{4}{8} = \dfrac{36}{}$

24. $\dfrac{}{3} = \dfrac{10}{15}$

25. $\dfrac{}{4} = \dfrac{18}{36}$

26. $\dfrac{2}{5} = \dfrac{18}{}$

27. $\dfrac{4}{} = \dfrac{16}{32}$

28. $\dfrac{4}{} = \dfrac{40}{60}$

29. $\dfrac{}{3} = \dfrac{8}{12}$

30. $\dfrac{2}{} = \dfrac{8}{16}$

Name: _____ **Date:** _____

Equivalent Fractions

Time:

:

Score:

/100

Complete the equivalent fractions.   2 points per question

(1) $\dfrac{3}{4} = \dfrac{}{24}$

(2) $\dfrac{1}{8} = \dfrac{}{56}$

(3) $\dfrac{}{4} = \dfrac{12}{16}$

(4) $\dfrac{}{5} = \dfrac{8}{10}$

(5) $\dfrac{4}{6} = \dfrac{32}{}$

(6) $\dfrac{1}{3} = \dfrac{}{6}$

(7) $\dfrac{}{8} = \dfrac{28}{56}$

(8) $\dfrac{1}{4} = \dfrac{9}{}$

(9) $\dfrac{1}{} = \dfrac{3}{18}$

(10) $\dfrac{}{3} = \dfrac{16}{24}$

(11) $\dfrac{2}{} = \dfrac{20}{50}$

(12) $\dfrac{}{8} = \dfrac{4}{32}$

(13) $\dfrac{1}{6} = \dfrac{}{24}$

(14) $\dfrac{2}{4} = \dfrac{}{28}$

(15) $\dfrac{2}{3} = \dfrac{4}{}$

(16) $\dfrac{4}{} = \dfrac{8}{12}$

(17) $\dfrac{1}{3} = \dfrac{}{27}$

(18) $\dfrac{7}{8} = \dfrac{}{48}$

(19) $\dfrac{4}{} = \dfrac{20}{25}$

(20) $\dfrac{1}{4} = \dfrac{8}{}$

Complete the equivalent fractions.

① $\frac{}{4} = \frac{15}{20}$ ② $\frac{4}{} = \frac{40}{60}$ ③ $\frac{}{3} = \frac{9}{27}$ ④ $\frac{1}{5} = \frac{}{25}$

⑤ $\frac{5}{8} = \frac{}{40}$ ⑥ $\frac{2}{3} = \frac{}{18}$ ⑦ $\frac{2}{8} = \frac{14}{}$ ⑧ $\frac{3}{6} = \frac{18}{}$

⑨ $\frac{3}{4} = \frac{21}{}$ ⑩ $\frac{2}{8} = \frac{8}{}$ ⑪ $\frac{4}{5} = \frac{16}{}$ ⑫ $\frac{3}{4} = \frac{27}{}$

⑬ $\frac{1}{3} = \frac{}{24}$ ⑭ $\frac{1}{6} = \frac{}{42}$ ⑮ $\frac{}{4} = \frac{10}{20}$ ⑯ $\frac{1}{3} = \frac{}{21}$

⑰ $\frac{}{8} = \frac{27}{72}$ ⑱ $\frac{1}{} = \frac{4}{16}$ ⑲ $\frac{4}{} = \frac{20}{30}$ ⑳ $\frac{6}{} = \frac{60}{80}$

㉑ $\frac{3}{} = \frac{21}{35}$ ㉒ $\frac{4}{8} = \frac{}{56}$ ㉓ $\frac{2}{6} = \frac{}{36}$ ㉔ $\frac{3}{5} = \frac{}{40}$

㉕ $\frac{1}{} = \frac{4}{12}$ ㉖ $\frac{}{6} = \frac{10}{12}$ ㉗ $\frac{4}{} = \frac{32}{40}$ ㉘ $\frac{1}{4} = \frac{3}{}$

㉙ $\frac{}{8} = \frac{49}{56}$ ㉚ $\frac{}{3} = \frac{6}{18}$

Name: —————————— Date: ——————

Fractions Addition

Time:

:

Score:

/100

Find the sum.

2 points per question

(1) $\dfrac{3}{9} + \dfrac{5}{6} =$

(2) $\dfrac{1}{9} + \dfrac{2}{10} =$

(3) $\dfrac{3}{6} + \dfrac{1}{2} =$

(4) $\dfrac{5}{7} + \dfrac{3}{4} =$

(5) $\dfrac{1}{8} + \dfrac{2}{3} =$

(6) $\dfrac{2}{5} + \dfrac{1}{11} =$

(7) $\dfrac{5}{7} + \dfrac{1}{6} =$

(8) $\dfrac{1}{3} + \dfrac{2}{4} =$

(9) $\dfrac{8}{9} + \dfrac{2}{9} =$

(10) $\dfrac{5}{9} + \dfrac{1}{6} =$

(11) $\dfrac{1}{6} + \dfrac{11}{12} =$

(12) $\dfrac{3}{4} + \dfrac{1}{5} =$

(13) $\dfrac{2}{3} + \dfrac{5}{9} =$

(14) $\dfrac{2}{3} + \dfrac{6}{12} =$

(15) $\dfrac{3}{6} + \dfrac{8}{10} =$

(16) $\dfrac{1}{2} + \dfrac{3}{6} =$

(17) $\dfrac{5}{8} + \dfrac{1}{2} =$

(18) $\dfrac{1}{3} + \dfrac{1}{3} =$

(19) $\dfrac{5}{8} + \dfrac{4}{5} =$

(20) $\dfrac{4}{5} + \dfrac{1}{4} =$

Find the sum.

① $\frac{1}{3} + \frac{3}{5} =$

② $\frac{6}{11} + \frac{1}{2} =$

③ $\frac{2}{6} + \frac{2}{12} =$

④ $\frac{8}{12} + \frac{3}{4} =$

⑤ $\frac{5}{9} + \frac{3}{6} =$

⑥ $\frac{2}{3} + \frac{5}{6} =$

⑦ $\frac{2}{5} + \frac{3}{12} =$

⑧ $\frac{2}{12} + \frac{1}{11} =$

⑨ $\frac{3}{4} + \frac{4}{5} =$

⑩ $\frac{8}{9} + \frac{1}{9} =$

⑪ $\frac{5}{10} + \frac{3}{4} =$

⑫ $\frac{2}{6} + \frac{8}{12} =$

⑬ $\frac{3}{9} + \frac{1}{3} =$

⑭ $\frac{1}{3} + \frac{1}{2} =$

⑮ $\frac{6}{8} + \frac{2}{8} =$

⑯ $\frac{1}{2} + \frac{1}{3} =$

⑰ $\frac{4}{9} + \frac{8}{10} =$

⑱ $\frac{3}{4} + \frac{1}{4} =$

⑲ $\frac{7}{8} + \frac{2}{6} =$

⑳ $\frac{1}{3} + \frac{2}{12} =$

㉑ $\frac{6}{11} + \frac{3}{8} =$

㉒ $\frac{1}{5} + \frac{3}{4} =$

㉓ $\frac{3}{6} + \frac{1}{2} =$

㉔ $\frac{6}{8} + \frac{4}{6} =$

㉕ $\frac{1}{9} + \frac{4}{9} =$

㉖ $\frac{1}{10} + \frac{1}{2} =$

㉗ $\frac{3}{8} + \frac{2}{12} =$

㉘ $\frac{7}{10} + \frac{4}{9} =$

㉙ $\frac{1}{3} + \frac{8}{10} =$

㉚ $\frac{7}{12} + \frac{1}{6} =$

Name: ———————————— Date: ————————

Fractions Addition

Time:

:

Score:

/100

Find the sum.

2 points per question

① $\dfrac{2}{3} + \dfrac{1}{3} =$

② $\dfrac{1}{8} + \dfrac{2}{5} =$

③ $\dfrac{2}{9} + \dfrac{3}{6} =$

④ $\dfrac{5}{6} + \dfrac{2}{3} =$

⑤ $\dfrac{1}{3} + \dfrac{4}{6} =$

⑥ $\dfrac{2}{7} + \dfrac{4}{6} =$

⑦ $\dfrac{1}{3} + \dfrac{1}{4} =$

⑧ $\dfrac{4}{6} + \dfrac{5}{8} =$

⑨ $\dfrac{8}{10} + \dfrac{2}{3} =$

⑩ $\dfrac{2}{4} + \dfrac{1}{4} =$

⑪ $\dfrac{1}{2} + \dfrac{1}{6} =$

⑫ $\dfrac{1}{2} + \dfrac{2}{4} =$

⑬ $\dfrac{5}{6} + \dfrac{1}{8} =$

⑭ $\dfrac{2}{3} + \dfrac{3}{8} =$

⑮ $\dfrac{1}{11} + \dfrac{4}{6} =$

⑯ $\dfrac{7}{9} + \dfrac{1}{4} =$

⑰ $\dfrac{4}{10} + \dfrac{1}{8} =$

⑱ $\dfrac{1}{4} + \dfrac{4}{5} =$

⑲ $\dfrac{3}{9} + \dfrac{4}{6} =$

⑳ $\dfrac{4}{7} + \dfrac{1}{6} =$

Find the sum.

1. $\dfrac{4}{6} + \dfrac{1}{3} =$

2. $\dfrac{1}{14} + \dfrac{3}{6} =$

3. $\dfrac{2}{9} + \dfrac{3}{6} =$

4. $\dfrac{4}{5} + \dfrac{2}{3} =$

5. $\dfrac{6}{16} + \dfrac{2}{3} =$

6. $\dfrac{3}{10} + \dfrac{6}{8} =$

7. $\dfrac{1}{3} + \dfrac{1}{5} =$

8. $\dfrac{1}{2} + \dfrac{3}{5} =$

9. $\dfrac{11}{14} + \dfrac{3}{4} =$

10. $\dfrac{5}{11} + \dfrac{1}{8} =$

11. $\dfrac{2}{12} + \dfrac{1}{3} =$

12. $\dfrac{2}{5} + \dfrac{2}{5} =$

13. $\dfrac{2}{3} + \dfrac{1}{4} =$

14. $\dfrac{13}{14} + \dfrac{2}{6} =$

15. $\dfrac{1}{10} + \dfrac{3}{5} =$

16. $\dfrac{8}{11} + \dfrac{1}{6} =$

17. $\dfrac{2}{5} + \dfrac{1}{3} =$

18. $\dfrac{7}{8} + \dfrac{1}{3} =$

19. $\dfrac{1}{12} + \dfrac{4}{5} =$

20. $\dfrac{3}{11} + \dfrac{2}{3} =$

21. $\dfrac{1}{2} + \dfrac{1}{5} =$

22. $\dfrac{2}{6} + \dfrac{4}{6} =$

23. $\dfrac{2}{12} + \dfrac{4}{6} =$

24. $\dfrac{7}{14} + \dfrac{1}{5} =$

25. $\dfrac{1}{5} + \dfrac{1}{6} =$

26. $\dfrac{2}{5} + \dfrac{1}{8} =$

27. $\dfrac{3}{6} + \dfrac{2}{4} =$

28. $\dfrac{11}{16} + \dfrac{2}{3} =$

29. $\dfrac{8}{14} + \dfrac{3}{5} =$

30. $\dfrac{2}{3} + \dfrac{2}{8} =$

Name: _____ Date: _____

Fractions Subtraction

Time:

:

Score:

/100

Find the difference.

2 points per question

(1) $\dfrac{1}{2} - \dfrac{2}{6} =$

(2) $\dfrac{6}{8} - \dfrac{3}{8} =$

(3) $\dfrac{3}{4} - \dfrac{2}{12} =$

(4) $\dfrac{5}{8} - \dfrac{2}{6} =$

(5) $\dfrac{4}{5} - \dfrac{2}{4} =$

(6) $\dfrac{5}{6} - \dfrac{3}{6} =$

(7) $\dfrac{5}{9} - \dfrac{1}{3} =$

(8) $\dfrac{4}{6} - \dfrac{5}{12} =$

(9) $\dfrac{6}{8} - \dfrac{2}{3} =$

(10) $\dfrac{7}{10} - \dfrac{1}{5} =$

(11) $\dfrac{2}{5} - \dfrac{2}{6} =$

(12) $\dfrac{1}{2} - \dfrac{5}{12} =$

(13) $\dfrac{2}{9} - \dfrac{1}{5} =$

(14) $\dfrac{7}{8} - \dfrac{2}{4} =$

(15) $\dfrac{2}{4} - \dfrac{3}{12} =$

(16) $\dfrac{3}{4} - \dfrac{1}{6} =$

(17) $\dfrac{6}{9} - \dfrac{2}{5} =$

(18) $\dfrac{3}{5} - \dfrac{1}{3} =$

(19) $\dfrac{2}{4} - \dfrac{1}{3} =$

(20) $\dfrac{2}{8} - \dfrac{1}{6} =$

Find the difference.

1. $\dfrac{1}{2} - \dfrac{3}{8} =$

2. $\dfrac{3}{5} - \dfrac{2}{4} =$

3. $\dfrac{5}{8} - \dfrac{1}{3} =$

4. $\dfrac{5}{10} - \dfrac{2}{8} =$

5. $\dfrac{3}{4} - \dfrac{1}{3} =$

6. $\dfrac{8}{10} - \dfrac{2}{3} =$

7. $\dfrac{3}{4} - \dfrac{1}{5} =$

8. $\dfrac{5}{6} - \dfrac{3}{4} =$

9. $\dfrac{11}{12} - \dfrac{1}{5} =$

10. $\dfrac{7}{8} - \dfrac{1}{4} =$

11. $\dfrac{2}{4} - \dfrac{1}{6} =$

12. $\dfrac{6}{8} - \dfrac{2}{3} =$

13. $\dfrac{7}{12} - \dfrac{2}{5} =$

14. $\dfrac{6}{9} - \dfrac{2}{4} =$

15. $\dfrac{3}{8} - \dfrac{1}{8} =$

16. $\dfrac{1}{2} - \dfrac{1}{5} =$

17. $\dfrac{4}{9} - \dfrac{1}{3} =$

18. $\dfrac{2}{9} - \dfrac{1}{6} =$

19. $\dfrac{3}{4} - \dfrac{2}{3} =$

20. $\dfrac{7}{10} - \dfrac{1}{5} =$

21. $\dfrac{4}{10} - \dfrac{1}{5} =$

22. $\dfrac{7}{8} - \dfrac{1}{3} =$

23. $\dfrac{2}{4} - \dfrac{1}{4} =$

24. $\dfrac{1}{2} - \dfrac{1}{3} =$

25. $\dfrac{3}{5} - \dfrac{2}{5} =$

26. $\dfrac{9}{10} - \dfrac{2}{4} =$

27. $\dfrac{10}{12} - \dfrac{2}{3} =$

28. $\dfrac{4}{8} - \dfrac{2}{5} =$

29. $\dfrac{6}{10} - \dfrac{2}{4} =$

30. $\dfrac{1}{2} - \dfrac{2}{6} =$

Name: ————————————— Date: ——————

Fractions Subtraction

Time:

:

Score:

/100

Find the difference.

2 points per question

(1) $\frac{1}{3} - \frac{1}{8} =$

(2) $\frac{4}{6} - \frac{1}{2} =$

(3) $\frac{1}{2} - \frac{1}{10} =$

(4) $\frac{2}{3} - \frac{2}{8} =$

(5) $\frac{3}{12} - \frac{2}{9} =$

(6) $\frac{7}{10} - \frac{2}{4} =$

(7) $\frac{7}{8} - \frac{4}{6} =$

(8) $\frac{1}{2} - \frac{2}{9} =$

(9) $\frac{6}{8} - \frac{2}{5} =$

(10) $\frac{8}{12} - \frac{2}{4} =$

(11) $\frac{1}{6} - \frac{1}{8} =$

(12) $\frac{4}{10} - \frac{1}{3} =$

(13) $\frac{2}{6} - \frac{1}{4} =$

(14) $\frac{3}{6} - \frac{1}{5} =$

(15) $\frac{2}{3} - \frac{5}{8} =$

(16) $\frac{5}{8} - \frac{1}{5} =$

(17) $\frac{2}{4} - \frac{1}{3} =$

(18) $\frac{3}{4} - \frac{3}{5} =$

(19) $\frac{7}{8} - \frac{2}{3} =$

(20) $\frac{3}{4} - \frac{1}{4} =$

Find the difference.

1) $\frac{3}{8} - \frac{2}{6} =$

2) $\frac{2}{6} - \frac{1}{4} =$

3) $\frac{2}{4} - \frac{1}{8} =$

4) $\frac{5}{6} - \frac{6}{9} =$

5) $\frac{5}{8} - \frac{2}{9} =$

6) $\frac{1}{3} - \frac{1}{5} =$

7) $\frac{3}{8} - \frac{1}{9} =$

8) $\frac{3}{4} - \frac{8}{12} =$

9) $\frac{2}{3} - \frac{1}{3} =$

10) $\frac{3}{8} - \frac{1}{5} =$

11) $\frac{1}{2} - \frac{1}{4} =$

12) $\frac{5}{6} - \frac{7}{9} =$

13) $\frac{2}{3} - \frac{3}{5} =$

14) $\frac{8}{10} - \frac{3}{5} =$

15) $\frac{1}{3} - \frac{1}{9} =$

16) $\frac{1}{2} - \frac{3}{8} =$

17) $\frac{8}{10} - \frac{2}{4} =$

18) $\frac{1}{2} - \frac{3}{9} =$

19) $\frac{7}{10} - \frac{2}{5} =$

20) $\frac{5}{8} - \frac{1}{12} =$

21) $\frac{3}{4} - \frac{2}{4} =$

22) $\frac{2}{4} - \frac{1}{9} =$

23) $\frac{1}{3} - \frac{1}{4} =$

24) $\frac{5}{6} - \frac{3}{4} =$

25) $\frac{5}{9} - \frac{2}{12} =$

26) $\frac{4}{5} - \frac{1}{5} =$

27) $\frac{3}{10} - \frac{1}{9} =$

28) $\frac{7}{9} - \frac{3}{12} =$

29) $\frac{3}{4} - \frac{3}{6} =$

30) $\frac{7}{8} - \frac{2}{8} =$

Name: ——————————— Date: ——————

Fractions Multiplication

Time:

:

Score:

/100

Find the product.

2 points per question

(1) $\dfrac{3}{5} \times \dfrac{3}{4} =$

(2) $\dfrac{1}{6} \times \dfrac{1}{5} =$

(3) $\dfrac{1}{12} \times \dfrac{6}{8} =$

(4) $\dfrac{2}{4} \times \dfrac{1}{6} =$

(5) $\dfrac{1}{2} \times \dfrac{2}{3} =$

(6) $\dfrac{1}{4} \times \dfrac{2}{8} =$

(7) $\dfrac{1}{3} \times \dfrac{3}{4} =$

(8) $\dfrac{6}{7} \times \dfrac{1}{6} =$

(9) $\dfrac{9}{10} \times \dfrac{4}{5} =$

(10) $\dfrac{6}{8} \times \dfrac{2}{8} =$

(11) $\dfrac{2}{5} \times \dfrac{1}{3} =$

(12) $\dfrac{3}{4} \times \dfrac{1}{3} =$

(13) $\dfrac{2}{7} \times \dfrac{3}{8} =$

(14) $\dfrac{6}{12} \times \dfrac{4}{5} =$

(15) $\dfrac{4}{10} \times \dfrac{4}{8} =$

(16) $\dfrac{3}{5} \times \dfrac{1}{3} =$

(17) $\dfrac{6}{8} \times \dfrac{2}{3} =$

(18) $\dfrac{1}{12} \times \dfrac{1}{4} =$

(19) $\dfrac{4}{9} \times \dfrac{4}{6} =$

(20) $\dfrac{3}{4} \times \dfrac{2}{3} =$

Find the product.

1. $\frac{3}{6} \times \frac{1}{3} =$

2. $\frac{3}{8} \times \frac{1}{8} =$

3. $\frac{1}{3} \times \frac{1}{4} =$

4. $\frac{3}{6} \times \frac{5}{6} =$

5. $\frac{3}{4} \times \frac{6}{13} =$

6. $\frac{5}{6} \times \frac{4}{8} =$

7. $\frac{1}{4} \times \frac{4}{6} =$

8. $\frac{4}{5} \times \frac{10}{11} =$

9. $\frac{1}{5} \times \frac{9}{10} =$

10. $\frac{3}{8} \times \frac{6}{7} =$

11. $\frac{1}{4} \times \frac{10}{13} =$

12. $\frac{4}{5} \times \frac{3}{7} =$

13. $\frac{5}{8} \times \frac{1}{2} =$

14. $\frac{2}{6} \times \frac{2}{6} =$

15. $\frac{2}{4} \times \frac{6}{9} =$

16. $\frac{1}{3} \times \frac{7}{10} =$

17. $\frac{2}{5} \times \frac{1}{5} =$

18. $\frac{1}{6} \times \frac{1}{4} =$

19. $\frac{2}{5} \times \frac{10}{12} =$

20. $\frac{1}{3} \times \frac{1}{5} =$

21. $\frac{1}{5} \times \frac{6}{9} =$

22. $\frac{2}{3} \times \frac{10}{13} =$

23. $\frac{4}{6} \times \frac{5}{6} =$

24. $\frac{4}{6} \times \frac{1}{2} =$

25. $\frac{4}{5} \times \frac{3}{13} =$

26. $\frac{1}{6} \times \frac{12}{14} =$

27. $\frac{1}{4} \times \frac{4}{7} =$

28. $\frac{1}{3} \times \frac{3}{4} =$

29. $\frac{2}{4} \times \frac{6}{8} =$

30. $\frac{4}{5} \times \frac{3}{8} =$

Name: _____ Date: _____

Fractions Multiplication

Time: :

Score: /100

Find the product.

2 points per question

1) $\dfrac{8}{9} \times \dfrac{2}{3} =$

2) $\dfrac{2}{8} \times \dfrac{1}{3} =$

3) $\dfrac{2}{7} \times \dfrac{4}{5} =$

4) $\dfrac{7}{11} \times \dfrac{3}{6} =$

5) $\dfrac{5}{10} \times \dfrac{1}{5} =$

6) $\dfrac{2}{9} \times \dfrac{2}{3} =$

7) $\dfrac{2}{4} \times \dfrac{2}{3} =$

8) $\dfrac{4}{6} \times \dfrac{3}{4} =$

9) $\dfrac{6}{10} \times \dfrac{1}{6} =$

10) $\dfrac{2}{5} \times \dfrac{1}{5} =$

11) $\dfrac{4}{11} \times \dfrac{2}{8} =$

12) $\dfrac{4}{7} \times \dfrac{1}{6} =$

13) $\dfrac{3}{9} \times \dfrac{3}{5} =$

14) $\dfrac{4}{6} \times \dfrac{2}{3} =$

15) $\dfrac{9}{10} \times \dfrac{2}{8} =$

16) $\dfrac{3}{4} \times \dfrac{1}{6} =$

17) $\dfrac{3}{7} \times \dfrac{4}{8} =$

18) $\dfrac{2}{3} \times \dfrac{4}{6} =$

19) $\dfrac{4}{5} \times \dfrac{1}{3} =$

20) $\dfrac{2}{10} \times \dfrac{2}{3} =$

Find the product.

① $\dfrac{2}{3} \times \dfrac{3}{5} =$

② $\dfrac{2}{9} \times \dfrac{8}{12} =$

③ $\dfrac{7}{8} \times \dfrac{3}{12} =$

④ $\dfrac{1}{6} \times \dfrac{1}{5} =$

⑤ $\dfrac{5}{12} \times \dfrac{3}{8} =$

⑥ $\dfrac{3}{4} \times \dfrac{3}{9} =$

⑦ $\dfrac{1}{7} \times \dfrac{1}{2} =$

⑧ $\dfrac{2}{5} \times \dfrac{1}{10} =$

⑨ $\dfrac{1}{3} \times \dfrac{2}{9} =$

⑩ $\dfrac{5}{8} \times \dfrac{1}{2} =$

⑪ $\dfrac{3}{7} \times \dfrac{1}{11} =$

⑫ $\dfrac{7}{9} \times \dfrac{1}{4} =$

⑬ $\dfrac{1}{6} \times \dfrac{5}{10} =$

⑭ $\dfrac{1}{5} \times \dfrac{3}{5} =$

⑮ $\dfrac{2}{10} \times \dfrac{1}{2} =$

⑯ $\dfrac{1}{5} \times \dfrac{10}{11} =$

⑰ $\dfrac{4}{6} \times \dfrac{1}{3} =$

⑱ $\dfrac{7}{8} \times \dfrac{4}{8} =$

⑲ $\dfrac{2}{3} \times \dfrac{1}{7} =$

⑳ $\dfrac{1}{4} \times \dfrac{3}{10} =$

㉑ $\dfrac{1}{4} \times \dfrac{3}{4} =$

㉒ $\dfrac{4}{12} \times \dfrac{4}{5} =$

㉓ $\dfrac{3}{5} \times \dfrac{5}{12} =$

㉔ $\dfrac{1}{2} \times \dfrac{6}{7} =$

㉕ $\dfrac{6}{9} \times \dfrac{1}{3} =$

㉖ $\dfrac{9}{10} \times \dfrac{8}{11} =$

㉗ $\dfrac{4}{9} \times \dfrac{2}{9} =$

㉘ $\dfrac{2}{3} \times \dfrac{1}{2} =$

㉙ $\dfrac{9}{11} \times \dfrac{2}{3} =$

㉚ $\dfrac{5}{8} \times \dfrac{6}{12} =$

Name: _____ Date: _____

Fractions Division

Time: :

Score: /100

Find the quotient.

2 points per question

① $\dfrac{1}{4} \div \dfrac{1}{3} =$

② $\dfrac{4}{7} \div \dfrac{1}{6} =$

③ $\dfrac{1}{2} \div \dfrac{5}{10} =$

④ $\dfrac{6}{12} \div \dfrac{3}{5} =$

⑤ $\dfrac{5}{12} \div \dfrac{1}{2} =$

⑥ $\dfrac{3}{6} \div \dfrac{4}{8} =$

⑦ $\dfrac{2}{4} \div \dfrac{2}{6} =$

⑧ $\dfrac{1}{3} \div \dfrac{2}{5} =$

⑨ $\dfrac{3}{9} \div \dfrac{4}{10} =$

⑩ $\dfrac{1}{6} \div \dfrac{4}{5} =$

⑪ $\dfrac{7}{10} \div \dfrac{1}{2} =$

⑫ $\dfrac{2}{4} \div \dfrac{2}{3} =$

⑬ $\dfrac{4}{5} \div \dfrac{5}{10} =$

⑭ $\dfrac{5}{9} \div \dfrac{3}{6} =$

⑮ $\dfrac{3}{12} \div \dfrac{2}{5} =$

⑯ $\dfrac{3}{6} \div \dfrac{1}{2} =$

⑰ $\dfrac{1}{2} \div \dfrac{2}{4} =$

⑱ $\dfrac{5}{7} \div \dfrac{2}{3} =$

⑲ $\dfrac{5}{10} \div \dfrac{4}{10} =$

⑳ $\dfrac{10}{12} \div \dfrac{1}{5} =$

Find the quotient.

(1) $\frac{2}{3} \div \frac{3}{5} =$

(2) $\frac{3}{9} \div \frac{1}{2} =$

(3) $\frac{6}{7} \div \frac{3}{7} =$

(4) $\frac{1}{2} \div \frac{1}{3} =$

(5) $\frac{1}{3} \div \frac{3}{9} =$

(6) $\frac{3}{6} \div \frac{1}{5} =$

(7) $\frac{1}{5} \div \frac{3}{6} =$

(8) $\frac{6}{9} \div \frac{4}{5} =$

(9) $\frac{3}{7} \div \frac{3}{7} =$

(10) $\frac{3}{4} \div \frac{1}{2} =$

(11) $\frac{4}{8} \div \frac{4}{7} =$

(12) $\frac{3}{4} \div \frac{1}{3} =$

(13) $\frac{4}{7} \div \frac{2}{8} =$

(14) $\frac{7}{9} \div \frac{2}{9} =$

(15) $\frac{1}{6} \div \frac{3}{4} =$

(16) $\frac{1}{3} \div \frac{3}{7} =$

(17) $\frac{6}{8} \div \frac{7}{8} =$

(18) $\frac{1}{4} \div \frac{6}{9} =$

(19) $\frac{6}{8} \div \frac{1}{2} =$

(20) $\frac{1}{6} \div \frac{1}{5} =$

(21) $\frac{1}{5} \div \frac{1}{8} =$

(22) $\frac{1}{3} \div \frac{1}{7} =$

(23) $\frac{1}{7} \div \frac{1}{2} =$

(24) $\frac{3}{8} \div \frac{1}{8} =$

(25) $\frac{2}{4} \div \frac{1}{6} =$

(26) $\frac{1}{2} \div \frac{6}{8} =$

(27) $\frac{4}{7} \div \frac{7}{9} =$

(28) $\frac{1}{2} \div \frac{1}{4} =$

(29) $\frac{7}{9} \div \frac{1}{2} =$

(30) $\frac{7}{8} \div \frac{4}{5} =$

Name: _____ Date: _____

Fractions Division

Time:

:

Score:

/100

Find the quotient.

2 points per question

① $\frac{1}{5} \div \frac{1}{4} =$

② $\frac{1}{2} \div \frac{1}{2} =$

③ $\frac{1}{4} \div \frac{6}{8} =$

④ $\frac{6}{8} \div \frac{4}{6} =$

⑤ $\frac{5}{9} \div \frac{2}{5} =$

⑥ $\frac{1}{2} \div \frac{2}{7} =$

⑦ $\frac{2}{6} \div \frac{1}{4} =$

⑧ $\frac{3}{5} \div \frac{2}{5} =$

⑨ $\frac{1}{2} \div \frac{3}{8} =$

⑩ $\frac{2}{3} \div \frac{1}{2} =$

⑪ $\frac{5}{10} \div \frac{7}{8} =$

⑫ $\frac{1}{4} \div \frac{2}{4} =$

⑬ $\frac{2}{5} \div \frac{1}{2} =$

⑭ $\frac{2}{3} \div \frac{4}{8} =$

⑮ $\frac{7}{9} \div \frac{3}{5} =$

⑯ $\frac{1}{2} \div \frac{1}{3} =$

⑰ $\frac{1}{2} \div \frac{2}{4} =$

⑱ $\frac{7}{10} \div \frac{1}{6} =$

⑲ $\frac{2}{8} \div \frac{2}{3} =$

⑳ $\frac{5}{6} \div \frac{2}{3} =$

Find the quotient.

1) $\dfrac{3}{4} \div \dfrac{1}{2} =$ 2) $\dfrac{2}{3} \div \dfrac{2}{3} =$ 3) $\dfrac{3}{6} \div \dfrac{6}{8} =$

4) $\dfrac{4}{5} \div \dfrac{1}{5} =$ 5) $\dfrac{2}{4} \div \dfrac{1}{4} =$ 6) $\dfrac{2}{3} \div \dfrac{1}{6} =$

7) $\dfrac{1}{3} \div \dfrac{4}{8} =$ 8) $\dfrac{1}{2} \div \dfrac{1}{2} =$ 9) $\dfrac{2}{5} \div \dfrac{4}{6} =$

10) $\dfrac{3}{4} \div \dfrac{1}{4} =$ 11) $\dfrac{1}{5} \div \dfrac{4}{8} =$ 12) $\dfrac{1}{3} \div \dfrac{7}{8} =$

13) $\dfrac{4}{5} \div \dfrac{1}{4} =$ 14) $\dfrac{3}{4} \div \dfrac{3}{5} =$ 15) $\dfrac{4}{6} \div \dfrac{2}{8} =$

16) $\dfrac{1}{2} \div \dfrac{3}{6} =$ 17) $\dfrac{3}{5} \div \dfrac{3}{6} =$ 18) $\dfrac{1}{2} \div \dfrac{7}{8} =$

19) $\dfrac{2}{5} \div \dfrac{2}{3} =$ 20) $\dfrac{5}{8} \div \dfrac{7}{8} =$ 21) $\dfrac{4}{6} \div \dfrac{1}{2} =$

22) $\dfrac{1}{2} \div \dfrac{1}{3} =$ 23) $\dfrac{2}{8} \div \dfrac{1}{2} =$ 24) $\dfrac{1}{3} \div \dfrac{1}{4} =$

25) $\dfrac{5}{6} \div \dfrac{2}{8} =$ 26) $\dfrac{1}{2} \div \dfrac{2}{5} =$ 27) $\dfrac{2}{5} \div \dfrac{2}{8} =$

28) $\dfrac{1}{2} \div \dfrac{4}{6} =$ 29) $\dfrac{1}{6} \div \dfrac{1}{3} =$ 30) $\dfrac{3}{6} \div \dfrac{1}{2} =$

15

Name: _____ **Date:** _____

Converting Mixed Numbers To Improper Fractions

Time: :

Score: /100

Convert.

2 points per question

① $6\frac{3}{4} =$

② $4\frac{1}{2} =$

③ $7\frac{2}{4} =$

④ $6\frac{2}{5} =$

⑤ $7\frac{1}{3} =$

⑥ $1\frac{1}{2} =$

⑦ $8\frac{2}{4} =$

⑧ $8\frac{1}{2} =$

⑨ $2\frac{3}{6} =$

⑩ $7\frac{1}{5} =$

⑪ $9\frac{1}{3} =$

⑫ $7\frac{4}{8} =$

⑬ $1\frac{5}{6} =$

⑭ $3\frac{2}{3} =$

⑮ $4\frac{4}{6} =$

⑯ $7\frac{1}{2} =$

⑰ $7\frac{2}{3} =$

⑱ $9\frac{2}{4} =$

⑲ $8\frac{1}{4} =$

⑳ $9\frac{5}{6} =$

Convert.

1. $4\frac{5}{16} =$

2. $2\frac{3}{6} =$

3. $4\frac{7}{8} =$

4. $3\frac{5}{6} =$

5. $3\frac{3}{4} =$

6. $2\frac{4}{6} =$

7. $2\frac{2}{6} =$

8. $1\frac{4}{6} =$

9. $6\frac{13}{18} =$

10. $7\frac{2}{4} =$

11. $5\frac{1}{9} =$

12. $8\frac{5}{8} =$

13. $2\frac{5}{6} =$

14. $7\frac{1}{2} =$

15. $6\frac{8}{12} =$

16. $3\frac{2}{4} =$

17. $5\frac{2}{18} =$

18. $3\frac{1}{3} =$

19. $2\frac{9}{12} =$

20. $2\frac{1}{2} =$

21. $6\frac{1}{4} =$

22. $1\frac{2}{5} =$

23. $3\frac{2}{16} =$

24. $5\frac{2}{4} =$

25. $7\frac{17}{18} =$

26. $7\frac{4}{12} =$

27. $5\frac{4}{8} =$

28. $4\frac{6}{10} =$

29. $2\frac{2}{4} =$

30. $4\frac{2}{4} =$

Name: ————————————— **Date:** ——————

Converting Mixed Numbers To Improper Fractions

Time:

:

Score:

/100

Convert.

2 points per question

① $9\frac{5}{6} =$

② $6\frac{1}{3} =$

③ $6\frac{3}{5} =$

④ $5\frac{4}{8} =$

⑤ $2\frac{1}{6} =$

⑥ $4\frac{1}{4} =$

⑦ $3\frac{1}{3} =$

⑧ $8\frac{4}{6} =$

⑨ $9\frac{2}{3} =$

⑩ $5\frac{2}{4} =$

⑪ $4\frac{3}{5} =$

⑫ $4\frac{2}{6} =$

⑬ $1\frac{3}{5} =$

⑭ $7\frac{7}{8} =$

⑮ $3\frac{3}{4} =$

⑯ $9\frac{1}{4} =$

⑰ $7\frac{1}{5} =$

⑱ $3\frac{5}{6} =$

⑲ $6\frac{2}{3} =$

⑳ $6\frac{4}{5} =$

Convert.

1. $9\frac{2}{4} =$ 2. $7\frac{2}{3} =$

3. $2\frac{4}{6} =$ 4. $2\frac{5}{6} =$

5. $6\frac{1}{4} =$ 6. $2\frac{2}{3} =$

7. $1\frac{7}{9} =$ 8. $8\frac{1}{5} =$

9. $3\frac{7}{8} =$ 10. $8\frac{2}{3} =$

11. $3\frac{4}{9} =$ 12. $7\frac{1}{2} =$

13. $5\frac{5}{8} =$ 14. $3\frac{3}{6} =$

15. $8\frac{1}{2} =$ 16. $7\frac{4}{5} =$

17. $5\frac{2}{4} =$ 18. $8\frac{1}{3} =$

19. $5\frac{2}{3} =$ 20. $1\frac{6}{8} =$

21. $6\frac{4}{5} =$ 22. $1\frac{1}{2} =$

23. $5\frac{7}{8} =$ 24. $3\frac{5}{9} =$

25. $5\frac{3}{5} =$ 26. $4\frac{1}{2} =$

27. $9\frac{5}{8} =$ 28. $6\frac{2}{4} =$

29. $4\frac{3}{9} =$ 30. $9\frac{2}{3} =$

Name: —————————————— Date: ————————

Converting Improper Fractions To Mixed Numbers

Time:

:

Score:

/100

Convert.

2 points per question

$\textcircled{1}$ $\dfrac{4}{3}$ =

$\textcircled{2}$ $\dfrac{22}{6}$ =

$\textcircled{3}$ $\dfrac{10}{4}$ =

$\textcircled{4}$ $\dfrac{25}{3}$ =

$\textcircled{5}$ $\dfrac{19}{3}$ =

$\textcircled{6}$ $\dfrac{46}{6}$ =

$\textcircled{7}$ $\dfrac{33}{4}$ =

$\textcircled{8}$ $\dfrac{31}{6}$ =

$\textcircled{9}$ $\dfrac{50}{6}$ =

$\textcircled{10}$ $\dfrac{11}{4}$ =

$\textcircled{11}$ $\dfrac{33}{8}$ =

$\textcircled{12}$ $\dfrac{6}{5}$ =

$\textcircled{13}$ $\dfrac{20}{6}$ =

$\textcircled{14}$ $\dfrac{7}{3}$ =

$\textcircled{15}$ $\dfrac{29}{3}$ =

$\textcircled{16}$ $\dfrac{37}{5}$ =

$\textcircled{17}$ $\dfrac{19}{6}$ =

$\textcircled{18}$ $\dfrac{11}{5}$ =

$\textcircled{19}$ $\dfrac{62}{8}$ =

$\textcircled{20}$ $\dfrac{29}{8}$ =

Convert.

1. $\dfrac{48}{5} =$

2. $\dfrac{25}{6} =$

3. $\dfrac{9}{8} =$

4. $\dfrac{22}{3} =$

5. $\dfrac{52}{6} =$

6. $\dfrac{22}{4} =$

7. $\dfrac{26}{3} =$

8. $\dfrac{29}{5} =$

9. $\dfrac{10}{4} =$

10. $\dfrac{28}{8} =$

11. $\dfrac{25}{8} =$

12. $\dfrac{16}{6} =$

13. $\dfrac{43}{5} =$

14. $\dfrac{29}{8} =$

15. $\dfrac{11}{4} =$

16. $\dfrac{10}{8} =$

17. $\dfrac{11}{3} =$

18. $\dfrac{49}{6} =$

19. $\dfrac{16}{3} =$

20. $\dfrac{23}{4} =$

21. $\dfrac{31}{4} =$

22. $\dfrac{36}{8} =$

23. $\dfrac{13}{3} =$

24. $\dfrac{37}{5} =$

25. $\dfrac{7}{4} =$

26. $\dfrac{20}{3} =$

27. $\dfrac{29}{6} =$

28. $\dfrac{46}{5} =$

29. $\dfrac{32}{6} =$

30. $\dfrac{39}{8} =$

Name: _____ Date: _____

Converting Improper Fractions To Mixed Numbers

Time:

:

Score:

/100

Convert.

2 points per question

① $\frac{9}{5}$ =

② $\frac{19}{2}$ =

③ $\frac{86}{9}$ =

④ $\frac{14}{8}$ =

⑤ $\frac{37}{4}$ =

⑥ $\frac{35}{9}$ =

⑦ $\frac{11}{5}$ =

⑧ $\frac{35}{6}$ =

⑨ $\frac{9}{2}$ =

⑩ $\frac{17}{3}$ =

⑪ $\frac{48}{5}$ =

⑫ $\frac{62}{8}$ =

⑬ $\frac{17}{2}$ =

⑭ $\frac{27}{4}$ =

⑮ $\frac{17}{8}$ =

⑯ $\frac{26}{3}$ =

⑰ $\frac{47}{5}$ =

⑱ $\frac{48}{9}$ =

⑲ $\frac{15}{4}$ =

⑳ $\frac{13}{3}$ =

Convert.

(1) $\frac{48}{5} =$

(2) $\frac{11}{3} =$

(3) $\frac{31}{8} =$

(4) $\frac{74}{9} =$

(5) $\frac{16}{5} =$

(6) $\frac{8}{5} =$

(7) $\frac{25}{3} =$

(8) $\frac{63}{8} =$

(9) $\frac{11}{2} =$

(10) $\frac{34}{6} =$

(11) $\frac{25}{4} =$

(12) $\frac{23}{3} =$

(13) $\frac{46}{5} =$

(14) $\frac{15}{6} =$

(15) $\frac{11}{5} =$

(16) $\frac{30}{4} =$

(17) $\frac{27}{5} =$

(18) $\frac{58}{8} =$

(19) $\frac{71}{9} =$

(20) $\frac{10}{3} =$

(21) $\frac{5}{2} =$

(22) $\frac{22}{3} =$

(23) $\frac{45}{6} =$

(24) $\frac{11}{4} =$

(25) $\frac{8}{3} =$

(26) $\frac{42}{9} =$

(27) $\frac{33}{8} =$

(28) $\frac{82}{9} =$

(29) $\frac{17}{2} =$

(30) $\frac{14}{8} =$

Name: ——————————— Date: ———————

Time:

:

Score:

/100

Fractions Identification

Color the fraction.

2 points per question

1) $\frac{3}{9}$ =

2) $\frac{3}{11}$ =

3) $\frac{1}{5}$ =

4) $\frac{1}{4}$ =

5) $\frac{1}{3}$ =

6) $\frac{5}{12}$ =

7) $\frac{3}{5}$ =

8) $\frac{1}{6}$ =

9) $\frac{9}{11}$ =

10) $\frac{2}{7}$ =

11) $\frac{4}{8}$ =

12) $\frac{1}{2}$ =

13) $\frac{2}{10}$ =

14) $\frac{1}{10}$ =

15) $\frac{2}{3}$ =

16) $\frac{4}{9}$ =

17) $\frac{8}{11}$ =

18) $\frac{3}{12}$ =

19) $\frac{5}{8}$ =

20) $\frac{4}{6}$ =

Identify the fraction.

1)  =

2) =

3)  =

4) =

5)  =

6) =

7)  =

8) =

9) =

10) =

11) =

12) =

13)  =

14) =

15)  =

16)  =

17)  =

18)  =

19)  =

20) 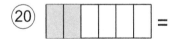 =

21)  =

22)  =

23)  =

24)  =

25)  =

26)  =

27) 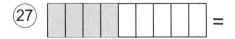 =

28) =

29)  =

30)  =

20 Name: —————————————— Date: ————

Time: : Score: /100

Fractions Identification

Color the fraction.

2 points per question

1) $\frac{5}{6}$ =

2) $\frac{3}{11}$ =

3) $\frac{3}{5}$ =

4) $\frac{5}{7}$ =

5) $\frac{2}{12}$ =

6) $\frac{2}{6}$ =

7) $\frac{1}{12}$ =

8) $\frac{4}{7}$ =

9) $\frac{2}{8}$ =

10) $\frac{1}{2}$ =

11) $\frac{2}{4}$ =

12) $\frac{5}{9}$ =

13) $\frac{2}{11}$ =

14) $\frac{1}{3}$ =

15) $\frac{4}{5}$ =

16) $\frac{1}{10}$ =

17) $\frac{2}{5}$ =

18) $\frac{7}{11}$ =

19) $\frac{4}{8}$ =

20) $\frac{6}{9}$ =

Identify the fraction.

1)  =   2) 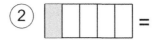 =

3)  =   4) 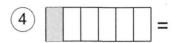 =

5)  =   6) =

7) 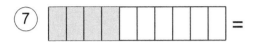 =   8) =

9)  =   10) =

11)  =   12) =

13)  =   14) =

15)  =   16) =

17)  =   18) =

19)  =   20) 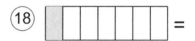 =

21) 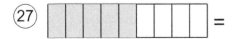 =   22) =

23) =   24) =

25) =   26) =

27) =   28) =

29) =   30) =

Name: ———————————— Date: ————————

Converting Fractions To Decimals

Time:

:

Score:

/100

Convert.

2 points per question

① $\frac{1}{2} =$

② $\frac{3}{5} =$

③ $\frac{1}{3} =$

④ $\frac{4}{6} =$

⑤ $\frac{5}{9} =$

⑥ $\frac{2}{3} =$

⑦ $\frac{3}{4} =$

⑧ $\frac{7}{9} =$

⑨ $\frac{5}{10} =$

⑩ $\frac{1}{5} =$

⑪ $\frac{1}{8} =$

⑫ $\frac{2}{8} =$

⑬ $\frac{2}{6} =$

⑭ $\frac{3}{10} =$

⑮ $\frac{2}{5} =$

⑯ $\frac{1}{4} =$

⑰ $\frac{6}{9} =$

⑱ $\frac{2}{10} =$

⑲ $\frac{3}{9} =$

⑳ $\frac{4}{8} =$

Convert.

① $\frac{3}{8}$ =

② $\frac{3}{5}$ =

③ $\frac{1}{2}$ =

④ $\frac{3}{4}$ =

⑤ $\frac{2}{9}$ =

⑥ $\frac{2}{6}$ =

⑦ $\frac{2}{3}$ =

⑧ $\frac{3}{10}$ =

⑨ $\frac{1}{8}$ =

⑩ $\frac{4}{8}$ =

⑪ $\frac{7}{10}$ =

⑫ $\frac{2}{4}$ =

⑬ $\frac{5}{6}$ =

⑭ $\frac{1}{10}$ =

⑮ $\frac{7}{9}$ =

⑯ $\frac{1}{5}$ =

⑰ $\frac{4}{5}$ =

⑱ $\frac{8}{9}$ =

⑲ $\frac{1}{3}$ =

⑳ $\frac{9}{10}$ =

㉑ $\frac{5}{8}$ =

㉒ $\frac{5}{10}$ =

㉓ $\frac{4}{6}$ =

㉔ $\frac{2}{5}$ =

㉕ $\frac{8}{10}$ =

㉖ $\frac{7}{8}$ =

㉗ $\frac{1}{4}$ =

㉘ $\frac{2}{8}$ =

㉙ $\frac{5}{9}$ =

㉚ $\frac{4}{9}$ =

Name: —————————————— **Date:** —————————

Time:
:

Score:
/100

Converting Fractions To Decimals

Convert.

2 points per question

(1) $\dfrac{1}{10}$ =

(2) $\dfrac{5}{6}$ =

(3) $\dfrac{3}{9}$ =

(4) $\dfrac{2}{5}$ =

(5) $\dfrac{3}{4}$ =

(6) $\dfrac{9}{10}$ =

(7) $\dfrac{2}{3}$ =

(8) $\dfrac{1}{2}$ =

(9) $\dfrac{4}{8}$ =

(10) $\dfrac{3}{10}$ =

(11) $\dfrac{2}{4}$ =

(12) $\dfrac{8}{9}$ =

(13) $\dfrac{4}{6}$ =

(14) $\dfrac{1}{3}$ =

(15) $\dfrac{1}{5}$ =

(16) $\dfrac{1}{8}$ =

(17) $\dfrac{5}{9}$ =

(18) $\dfrac{5}{8}$ =

(19) $\dfrac{3}{6}$ =

(20) $\dfrac{4}{5}$ =

Convert.

1) $\dfrac{1}{4} =$ 2) $\dfrac{4}{9} =$ 3) $\dfrac{1}{6} =$

4) $\dfrac{3}{5} =$ 5) $\dfrac{3}{10} =$ 6) $\dfrac{1}{2} =$

7) $\dfrac{1}{3} =$ 8) $\dfrac{4}{6} =$ 9) $\dfrac{7}{8} =$

10) $\dfrac{5}{10} =$ 11) $\dfrac{2}{4} =$ 12) $\dfrac{6}{9} =$

13) $\dfrac{3}{6} =$ 14) $\dfrac{2}{9} =$ 15) $\dfrac{6}{10} =$

16) $\dfrac{3}{9} =$ 17) $\dfrac{4}{8} =$ 18) $\dfrac{4}{10} =$

19) $\dfrac{5}{8} =$ 20) $\dfrac{2}{3} =$ 21) $\dfrac{2}{10} =$

22) $\dfrac{3}{4} =$ 23) $\dfrac{2}{5} =$ 24) $\dfrac{5}{9} =$

25) $\dfrac{1}{10} =$ 26) $\dfrac{4}{5} =$ 27) $\dfrac{2}{8} =$

28) $\dfrac{6}{8} =$ 29) $\dfrac{1}{5} =$ 30) $\dfrac{7}{10} =$

Name: _____ Date: _____

Decimal Addition

Time:

:

Score:

/100

Add.

2 points per question

①   0.085
    + 0.014
    _____

②   0.05
    + 1.62
    _____

③   0.41
    + 0.01
    _____

④   0.2
    + 3.2
    _____

⑤   0.03
    + 1.49
    _____

⑥   0.005
    + 0.023
    _____

⑦   8.6
    + 16.2
    _____

⑧   0.4
    + 18.2
    _____

⑨   0.05
    + 1.68
    _____

⑩   0.054
    + 0.056
    _____

⑪   0.007
    + 0.061
    _____

⑫   4.9
    + 5.8
    _____

⑬   8.6
    + 15.1
    _____

⑭   3.6
    + 3.3
    _____

⑮   0.039
    + 0.124
    _____

⑯   0.9
    + 16.1
    _____

⑰   3.7
    + 10.1
    _____

⑱   0.05
    + 1.38
    _____

⑲   0.031
    + 0.082
    _____

⑳   0.09
    + 1.96
    _____

Add.

① 14.4
  + 6.8

② 1.64
  + 0.14

③ 12.2
  + 5.9

④ 16.6
  + 0.4

⑤ 8.3
  + 7.4

⑥ 14.5
  + 9.0

⑦ 16.4
  + 5.8

⑧ 15.6
  + 6.6

⑨ 15.4
  + 4.6

⑩ 0.119
  + 0.049

⑪ 1.59
  + 0.93

⑫ 19.5
  + 4.9

⑬ 10.7
  + 4.9

⑭ 0.079
  + 0.044

⑮ 0.048
  + 0.011

⑯ 0.124
  + 0.003

⑰ 0.82
  + 0.95

⑱ 13.6
  + 4.0

⑲ 0.118
  + 0.021

⑳ 7.6
  + 4.7

㉑ 10.4
  + 0.9

㉒ 0.067
  + 0.034

㉓ 1.90
  + 0.47

㉔ 0.068
  + 0.022

㉕ 8.6
  + 9.7

㉖ 0.82
  + 0.85

㉗ 0.94
  + 0.98

㉘ 0.82
  + 0.79

㉙ 1.40
  + 0.34

㉚ 12.1
  + 1.3

Name: ——————————— Date: ————————

Decimal Addition

Add.   2 points per question

(1)   1.5
    + 1.3

(2)   0.5
    + 0.8

(3)   0.11
    + 0.07

(4)   0.06
    + 0.13

(5)   0.08
    + 0.09

(6)   0.003
    + 0.006

(7)   0.012
    + 0.003

(8)   0.6
    + 0.8

(9)   0.002
    + 0.013

(10)   0.6
    + 2.0

(11)   0.6
    + 1.4

(12)   0.06
    + 0.03

(13)   0.11
    + 0.20

(14)   1.7
    + 1.4

(15)   0.006
    + 0.004

(16)   0.019
    + 0.009

(17)   1.2
    + 1.8

(18)   0.8
    + 1.2

(19)   0.018
    + 0.018

(20)   0.1
    + 0.7

Add.

1. 0.11
   + 0.10

2. 0.005
   + 0.020

3. 0.009
   + 0.019

4. 0.10
   + 0.05

5. 0.03
   + 0.04

6. 0.019
   + 0.019

7. 1.6
   + 1.1

8. 1.3
   + 0.6

9. 0.12
   + 0.01

10. 0.08
    + 0.02

11. 0.5
    + 1.0

12. 0.9
    + 1.2

13. 0.001
    + 0.004

14. 0.011
    + 0.008

15. 0.002
    + 0.017

16. 0.6
    + 0.4

17. 1.7
    + 0.8

18. 1.7
    + 1.0

19. 0.001
    + 0.017

20. 0.6
    + 0.7

21. 0.011
    + 0.004

22. 0.019
    + 0.011

23. 0.019
    + 0.005

24. 1.8
    + 1.7

25. 0.006
    + 0.003

26. 0.006
    + 0.011

27. 0.012
    + 0.004

28. 1.1
    + 1.6

29. 0.008
    + 0.019

30. 0.018
    + 0.009

25 Name: —————————————— Date: ——————

Decimal Subtraction

Time:

:

Score:

/100

2 points per question

Subtract.

① 0.67
  - 0.29

② 0.051
  - 0.021

③ 0.56
  - 0.41

④ 8.5
  - 7.6

⑤ 8.0
  - 3.2

⑥ 0.086
  - 0.060

⑦ 0.80
  - 0.72

⑧ 0.45
  - 0.21

⑨ 7.2
  - 5.8

⑩ 8.1
  - 3.7

⑪ 0.082
  - 0.075

⑫ 0.51
  - 0.04

⑬ 0.043
  - 0.016

⑭ 0.75
  - 0.66

⑮ 0.077
  - 0.025

⑯ 5.2
  - 4.9

⑰ 2.0
  - 0.1

⑱ 3.9
  - 1.5

⑲ 0.75
  - 0.29

⑳ 0.61
  - 0.50

Subtract.

1) 0.17
  - 0.05

2) 0.15
  - 0.12

3) 0.015
  - 0.009

4) 0.006
  - 0.001

5) 0.016
  - 0.014

6) 0.04
  - 0.02

7) 0.17
  - 0.10

8) 1.3
  - 0.3

9) 0.14
  - 0.04

10) 0.20
  - 0.12

11) 0.12
  - 0.06

12) 0.016
  - 0.010

13) 1.8
  - 0.1

14) 0.14
  - 0.01

15) 0.009
  - 0.008

16) 1.8
  - 0.5

17) 0.18
  - 0.09

18) 0.08
  - 0.06

19) 1.9
  - 1.1

20) 0.15
  - 0.07

21) 0.12
  - 0.04

22) 1.2
  - 0.5

23) 0.012
  - 0.002

24) 0.011
  - 0.006

25) 1.5
  - 0.5

26) 0.19
  - 0.12

27) 1.1
  - 0.2

28) 0.17
  - 0.03

29) 0.18
  - 0.14

30) 0.7
  - 0.4

26 Name: _____ Date: _____

Decimal Subtraction

Time:
:

Score:
/100

Subtract.

2 points per question

① 13.9
- 6.2

② 0.091
- 0.006

③ 0.180
- 0.158

④ 1.60
- 0.41

⑤ 0.98
- 0.72

⑥ 15.8
- 5.0

⑦ 0.165
- 0.024

⑧ 1.74
- 0.05

⑨ 1.20
- 0.69

⑩ 13.3
- 11.0

⑪ 19.8
- 5.3

⑫ 1.19
- 1.14

⑬ 0.117
- 0.038

⑭ 0.195
- 0.003

⑮ 0.180
- 0.143

⑯ 1.78
- 0.54

⑰ 1.49
- 1.13

⑱ 17.2
- 2.5

⑲ 14.4
- 12.9

⑳ 1.81
- 1.81

Subtract.

① 4.9
  - 4.6

② 0.97
  - 0.20

③ 0.11
  - 0.09

④ 9.9
  - 3.3

⑤ 6.0
  - 4.8

⑥ 0.97
  - 0.03

⑦ 9.5
  - 6.9

⑧ 6.5
  - 1.9

⑨ 0.41
  - 0.18

⑩ 0.99
  - 0.40

⑪ 2.1
  - 2.1

⑫ 9.8
  - 9.8

⑬ 0.68
  - 0.21

⑭ 2.3
  - 1.8

⑮ 0.75
  - 0.56

⑯ 0.36
  - 0.14

⑰ 0.65
  - 0.22

⑱ 0.82
  - 0.45

⑲ 0.33
  - 0.23

⑳ 0.37
  - 0.16

㉑ 4.2
  - 0.2

㉒ 0.82
  - 0.75

㉓ 7.1
  - 5.9

㉔ 6.8
  - 2.9

㉕ 5.0
  - 2.5

㉖ 5.3
  - 2.5

㉗ 4.3
  - 1.7

㉘ 0.74
  - 0.54

㉙ 9.5
  - 6.1

㉚ 8.8
  - 7.6

Name: —————————— Date: ——————

Decimal Multiplication: 1-digit and 2-Digit Numbers

Time:

:

Score:

/100

2 points per question

Multiply.

1)
  8
× 0.4

2)
  4
× 0.5

3)
  9
× 0.1

4)
  4
× 0.7

5)
  1
× 3.7

6)
  3
× 2.7

7)
  7
× 0.6

8)
  2
× 4.3

9)
  3
× 4.0

10)
  6
× 4.4

11)
  1
× 1.1

12)
  9
× 5.5

13)
  9
× 0.6

14)
  8
× 0.6

15)
  7
× 7.8

16)
  4
× 0.2

17)
  7
× 0.2

18)
  6
× 0.4

19)
  5
× 0.6

20)
  6
× 8.1

Multiply.

① 2
× 3.8

② 4
× 0.4

③ 2
× 8.6

④ 5
× 5.4

⑤ 7
× 0.2

⑥ 1
× 7.9

⑦ 6
× 0.1

⑧ 4
× 0.6

⑨ 4
× 5.6

⑩ 1
× 6.8

⑪ 1
× 2.7

⑫ 3
× 0.2

⑬ 1
× 4.1

⑭ 8
× 1.3

⑮ 7
× 1.5

⑯ 9
× 8.6

⑰ 3
× 0.8

⑱ 3
× 0.5

⑲ 6
× 3.4

⑳ 6
× 1.8

㉑ 2
× 7.0

㉒ 1
× 8.0

㉓ 5
× 0.5

㉔ 7
× 4.6

㉕ 7
× 8.9

㉖ 6
× 0.3

㉗ 3
× 1.6

㉘ 6
× 6.1

㉙ 8
× 7.3

㉚ 8
× 0.6

Name: —————————————— Date: ——————

Decimal Multiplication: 1-digit and 2-Digit Numbers

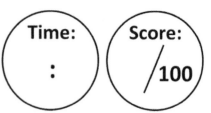

Time:

:

Score:

/100

2 points per question

Multiply.

(1)
```
    3
×  4.7
```

(2)
```
    3
×  3.5
```

(3)
```
    3
×  0.3
```

(4)
```
    4
×  3.5
```

(5)
```
    2
×  1.9
```

(6)
```
    4
×  1.4
```

(7)
```
    8
×  0.5
```

(8)
```
    4
×  0.7
```

(9)
```
    6
×  0.0
```

(10)
```
    5
×  0.8
```

(11)
```
    3
×  0.7
```

(12)
```
    3
×  3.8
```

(13)
```
    6
×  0.8
```

(14)
```
    3
×  1.3
```

(15)
```
    8
×  6.5
```

(16)
```
    4
×  3.1
```

(17)
```
    3
×  7.2
```

(18)
```
    7
×  0.0
```

(19)
```
    1
×  7.5
```

(20)
```
    1
×  0.4
```

Multiply.

① 2 × 0.0	② 6 × 3.6	③ 9 × 7.5	④ 4 × 0.0	⑤ 4 × 3.6
⑥ 6 × 0.7	⑦ 9 × 0.1	⑧ 8 × 0.6	⑨ 4 × 2.9	⑩ 9 × 0.8
⑪ 1 × 3.4	⑫ 5 × 0.8	⑬ 4 × 8.1	⑭ 1 × 0.1	⑮ 5 × 0.6
⑯ 5 × 0.3	⑰ 8 × 0.5	⑱ 8 × 5.6	⑲ 1 × 0.4	⑳ 4 × 6.9
㉑ 4 × 5.3	㉒ 5 × 0.4	㉓ 4 × 8.5	㉔ 5 × 6.6	㉕ 9 × 1.5
㉖ 6 × 0.8	㉗ 5 × 0.2	㉘ 6 × 0.1	㉙ 6 × 1.2	㉚ 9 × 3.8

Name: ——————————— Date: ————————

Decimal Multiplication: 3-digit Numbers By 2-Digit Numbers

Time:

:

Score:

/100

2 points per question

Multiply.

① 0.31
× 1.0

② 9.2
× 0.16

③ 1.1
× 65

④ 36
× 0.69

⑤ 34
× 9.5

⑥ 76
× 69

⑦ 0.73
× 100

⑧ 1.6
× 28

⑨ 0.70
× 0.05

⑩ 0.2
× 11

⑪ 21
× 0.83

⑫ 0.7
× 5.7

⑬ 0.45
× 0.55

⑭ 5
× 0.59

⑮ 0.73
× 6.0

⑯ 0.56
× 3.0

⑰ 35
× 67

⑱ 26
× 1.4

⑲ 49
× 7.0

⑳ 0.84
× 60

Multiply.

1)
$$\begin{array}{r} 0.47 \\ \times\ \ 22 \\ \hline \end{array}$$

2)
$$\begin{array}{r} 1 \\ \times\ 0.57 \\ \hline \end{array}$$

3)
$$\begin{array}{r} 3.7 \\ \times\ \ 80 \\ \hline \end{array}$$

4)
$$\begin{array}{r} 1 \\ \times\ 0.28 \\ \hline \end{array}$$

5)
$$\begin{array}{r} 84 \\ \times\ 0.23 \\ \hline \end{array}$$

6)
$$\begin{array}{r} 0.2 \\ \times\ 8.0 \\ \hline \end{array}$$

7)
$$\begin{array}{r} 6.8 \\ \times\ 0.57 \\ \hline \end{array}$$

8)
$$\begin{array}{r} 0.02 \\ \times\ 9.9 \\ \hline \end{array}$$

9)
$$\begin{array}{r} 0.59 \\ \times\ \ \ 9 \\ \hline \end{array}$$

10)
$$\begin{array}{r} 90 \\ \times\ 22 \\ \hline \end{array}$$

11)
$$\begin{array}{r} 74 \\ \times\ 0.66 \\ \hline \end{array}$$

12)
$$\begin{array}{r} 43 \\ \times\ 0.76 \\ \hline \end{array}$$

13)
$$\begin{array}{r} 1.2 \\ \times\ \ 25 \\ \hline \end{array}$$

14)
$$\begin{array}{r} 6 \\ \times\ 1.7 \\ \hline \end{array}$$

15)
$$\begin{array}{r} 0.19 \\ \times\ 0.20 \\ \hline \end{array}$$

16)
$$\begin{array}{r} 49 \\ \times\ 0.19 \\ \hline \end{array}$$

17)
$$\begin{array}{r} 5.2 \\ \times\ \ 28 \\ \hline \end{array}$$

18)
$$\begin{array}{r} 0.90 \\ \times\ \ \ 72 \\ \hline \end{array}$$

19)
$$\begin{array}{r} 4 \\ \times\ 67 \\ \hline \end{array}$$

20)
$$\begin{array}{r} 54 \\ \times\ 0.47 \\ \hline \end{array}$$

21)
$$\begin{array}{r} 0.64 \\ \times\ \ 87 \\ \hline \end{array}$$

22)
$$\begin{array}{r} 4.8 \\ \times\ 5.0 \\ \hline \end{array}$$

23)
$$\begin{array}{r} 4.6 \\ \times\ 1.9 \\ \hline \end{array}$$

24)
$$\begin{array}{r} 38 \\ \times\ 0.62 \\ \hline \end{array}$$

25)
$$\begin{array}{r} 0.97 \\ \times\ \ 4.9 \\ \hline \end{array}$$

26)
$$\begin{array}{r} 5.7 \\ \times\ 1.4 \\ \hline \end{array}$$

27)
$$\begin{array}{r} 0.64 \\ \times\ 0.99 \\ \hline \end{array}$$

28)
$$\begin{array}{r} 3.6 \\ \times\ 8.1 \\ \hline \end{array}$$

29)
$$\begin{array}{r} 79 \\ \times\ 0.25 \\ \hline \end{array}$$

30)
$$\begin{array}{r} 0.46 \\ \times\ \ 13 \\ \hline \end{array}$$

Name: _____ Date: _____

Decimal Multiplication: 3-digit Numbers By 2-Digit Numbers

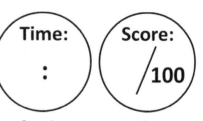

Time:

:

Score:

/100

2 points per question

Multiply.

(1)
```
      8
 ×   24
```

(2)
```
     29
 ×  2.5
```

(3)
```
   0.98
 ×  1.2
```

(4)
```
   0.82
 × 0.49
```

(5)
```
    1.7
 × 0.73
```

(6)
```
     56
 × 0.62
```

(7)
```
     55
 ×   66
```

(8)
```
     27
 × 0.31
```

(9)
```
    5.7
 × 0.25
```

(10)
```
    6.4
 × 0.57
```

(11)
```
    5.2
 × 0.04
```

(12)
```
    4.1
 ×  1.5
```

(13)
```
     82
 × 0.32
```

(14)
```
   0.91
 × 0.15
```

(15)
```
     79
 ×   56
```

(16)
```
     44
 ×   49
```

(17)
```
    3.4
 ×  6.0
```

(18)
```
     75
 ×  8.5
```

(19)
```
     15
 ×  1.2
```

(20)
```
   0.38
 ×  8.8
```

Multiply.

① 68 × 83	② 44 × 42	③ 0.91 × 6.4	④ 37 × 3.0
⑤ 0.05 × 0.91	⑥ 4 × 0.50	⑦ 0.27 × 7.8	⑧ 0.32 × 94
⑨ 4 × 8.2	⑩ 0.68 × 2.7	⑪ 3.5 × 83	⑫ 75 × 0.54
⑬ 60 × 0.59	⑭ 9 × 0.90	⑮ 0.36 × 0.72	⑯ 0.19 × 0.85
⑰ 0.48 × 9.5	⑱ 3.5 × 0.14	⑲ 0.92 × 5.6	⑳ 0.84 × 17
㉑ 4 × 0.97	㉒ 7.1 × 0.96	㉓ 55 × 2.3	㉔ 5.4 × 15
㉕ 9.4 × 96	㉖ 45 × 0.79	㉗ 0.10 × 6.3	㉘ 0.08 × 8.4
㉙ 1.0 × 0.90	㉚ 8.2 × 33		

Name: —————————————— Date: ——————

Decimal Division with 3-digit Numbers

Time:

:

Score:

/100

Find the quotient.

2 points per question

1) $9\overline{)8.56}$

2) $2\overline{)5.19}$

3) $5\overline{)0.44}$

4) $5\overline{)6.87}$

5) $1\overline{)0.24}$

6) $1\overline{)5.44}$

7) $6\overline{)0.86}$

8) $8\overline{)0.23}$

9) $4\overline{)9.02}$

10) $7\overline{)9.13}$

11) $7\overline{)8.72}$

12) $7\overline{)3.84}$

13) $7\overline{)0.92}$

14) $5\overline{)6.80}$

15) $6\overline{)0.51}$

16) $4\overline{)0.64}$

17) $9\overline{)8.45}$

18) $8\overline{)2.79}$

19) $8\overline{)7.71}$

20) $4\overline{)4.08}$

Find the quotient.

① $2 \overline{)\, 8.77}$ ② $8 \overline{)\, 8.46}$ ③ $6 \overline{)\, 9.17}$ ④ $4 \overline{)\, 7.09}$ ⑤ $3 \overline{)\, 8.55}$

⑥ $5 \overline{)\, 7.26}$ ⑦ $9 \overline{)\, 8.29}$ ⑧ $4 \overline{)\, 8.37}$ ⑨ $4 \overline{)\, 0.38}$ ⑩ $7 \overline{)\, 0.75}$

⑪ $5 \overline{)\, 9.64}$ ⑫ $8 \overline{)\, 3.17}$ ⑬ $10 \overline{)\, 2.66}$ ⑭ $3 \overline{)\, 0.66}$ ⑮ $9 \overline{)\, 4.88}$

⑯ $4 \overline{)\, 8.04}$ ⑰ $5 \overline{)\, 5.19}$ ⑱ $6 \overline{)\, 9.72}$ ⑲ $6 \overline{)\, 0.04}$ ⑳ $2 \overline{)\, 9.28}$

㉑ $2 \overline{)\, 0.12}$ ㉒ $3 \overline{)\, 2.31}$ ㉓ $5 \overline{)\, 0.37}$ ㉔ $4 \overline{)\, 3.72}$ ㉕ $7 \overline{)\, 0.65}$

㉖ $6 \overline{)\, 2.87}$ ㉗ $5 \overline{)\, 9.11}$ ㉘ $5 \overline{)\, 0.44}$ ㉙ $2 \overline{)\, 8.19}$ ㉚ $9 \overline{)\, 5.71}$

Name: _____ **Date:** _____

Decimal Division with 3-digit Numbers

Time:

:

Score:

 /100

Find the quotient.

2 points per question

1) $3\overline{)0.25}$

2) $8\overline{)6.25}$

3) $1\overline{)2.36}$

4) $5\overline{)5.08}$

5) $6\overline{)0.26}$

6) $7\overline{)8.52}$

7) $1\overline{)5.27}$

8) $4\overline{)1.54}$

9) $3\overline{)0.58}$

10) $4\overline{)9.46}$

11) $6\overline{)2.89}$

12) $6\overline{)0.11}$

13) $3\overline{)0.62}$

14) $4\overline{)2.24}$

15) $9\overline{)0.31}$

16) $2\overline{)0.74}$

17) $3\overline{)0.04}$

18) $5\overline{)3.45}$

19) $8\overline{)1.35}$

20) $9\overline{)8.59}$

Find the quotient.

① $5\overline{)0.67}$ ② $2\overline{)7.56}$ ③ $7\overline{)0.24}$ ④ $6\overline{)9.87}$ ⑤ $8\overline{)0.35}$

⑥ $8\overline{)7.34}$ ⑦ $4\overline{)0.92}$ ⑧ $9\overline{)0.41}$ ⑨ $9\overline{)4.38}$ ⑩ $8\overline{)5.12}$

⑪ $1\overline{)5.33}$ ⑫ $2\overline{)6.34}$ ⑬ $7\overline{)8.23}$ ⑭ $10\overline{)0.73}$ ⑮ $5\overline{)0.29}$

⑯ $2\overline{)8.56}$ ⑰ $5\overline{)1.58}$ ⑱ $7\overline{)85}$ ⑲ $6\overline{)0.30}$ ⑳ $2\overline{)2.30}$

㉑ $5\overline{)8.88}$ ㉒ $7\overline{)7.66}$ ㉓ $5\overline{)5.65}$ ㉔ $3\overline{)0.41}$ ㉕ $1\overline{)1.22}$

㉖ $6\overline{)0.21}$ ㉗ $4\overline{)8.43}$ ㉘ $7\overline{)4.06}$ ㉙ $7\overline{)8.82}$ ㉚ $6\overline{)0.34}$

33 Name: _____ Date: _____

Decimal Division with Decimal Divisors

Time: :

Score: /100

Find the quotient.

2 points per question

① 3.6) 0.12

② 22.7) 5.1

③ 85.0) 1.6

④ 6.93) 0.48

⑤ 9.96) 0.02

⑥ 35.2) 0.89

⑦ 10.3) 0.65

⑧ 5.20) 1.0

⑨ 2.20) 0.90

⑩ 63.2) 6.69

⑪ 4.76) 1.06

⑫ 3.26) 8.7

⑬ 4.22) 0.22

⑭ 50.9) 0.97

⑮ 0.31) 0.100

⑯ 3.06) 0.1

⑰ 45.5) 5.1

⑱ 0.41) 0.014

⑲ 4.80) 8.2

⑳ 1.13) 0.019

Find the quotient.

(1) $2.63\overline{)7.1}$

(2) $85.9\overline{)0.057}$

(3) $25.5\overline{)0.036}$

(4) $8.89\overline{)0.071}$

(5) $88.2\overline{)0.002}$

(6) $8.37\overline{)16}$

(7) $0.56\overline{)0.50}$

(8) $3.06\overline{)9.2}$

(9) $8.17\overline{)0.93}$

(10) $2.99\overline{)0.046}$

(11) $70.5\overline{)0.59}$

(12) $5.04\overline{)0.48}$

(13) $2.17\overline{)1.2}$

(14) $7.30\overline{)0.024}$

(15) $59.0\overline{)0.013}$

(16) $4.86\overline{)3.7}$

(17) $6.06\overline{)6.2}$

(18) $8.55\overline{)1.2}$

(19) $2.27\overline{)0.76}$

(20) $89.6\overline{)8.9}$

(21) $6.19\overline{)0.036}$

(22) $7.29\overline{)0.013}$

(23) $26.4\overline{)0.075}$

(24) $73.5\overline{)5.4}$

(25) $7.8\overline{)0.02}$

(26) $9.24\overline{)0.014}$

(27) $3.77\overline{)8.1}$

(28) $6.39\overline{)0.47}$

(29) $6.2\overline{)0.78}$

(30) $14.3\overline{)0.074}$

Name: _____ Date: _____

Decimal Division with Decimal Divisors

Time: :

Score: /100

Find the quotient.

2 points per question

① 65.5⟌0.92

② 5.75⟌0.60

③ 62.9⟌0.84

④ 3.82⟌0.83

⑤ 49.7⟌0.59

⑥ 8.56⟌0.051

⑦ 6.05⟌5.56

⑧ 14.8⟌4.7

⑨ 9.95⟌3.02

⑩ 8.56⟌0.46

⑪ 8.87⟌0.81

⑫ 9.51⟌6.8

⑬ 10.6⟌0.024

⑭ 12.1⟌0.78

⑮ 1.001⟌9.0

⑯ 87.8⟌0.001

⑰ 59.0⟌0.048

⑱ 3.16⟌0.92

⑲ 2.55⟌1.8

⑳ 2.32⟌0.022

Find the quotient.

① $1.68\overline{)8.7}$ ② $3.8\overline{)3.02}$ ③ $27.4\overline{)1.59}$ ④ $2.90\overline{)0.031}$ ⑤ $18.4\overline{)7.9}$

⑥ $0.77\overline{)8.1}$ ⑦ $0.3\overline{)1.7}$ ⑧ $8.3\overline{)5.5}$ ⑨ $8.5\overline{)51}$ ⑩ $0.24\overline{)5.3}$

⑪ $2.28\overline{)2.50}$ ⑫ $1.02\overline{)0.061}$ ⑬ $1.53\overline{)0.95}$ ⑭ $1.48\overline{)8.8}$ ⑮ $8.7\overline{)9.5}$

⑯ $29.8\overline{)1.6}$ ⑰ $2.15\overline{)8.5}$ ⑱ $2.13\overline{)0.083}$ ⑲ $22.6\overline{)9.6}$ ⑳ $5.9\overline{)9.3}$

㉑ $27.8\overline{)0.025}$ ㉒ $17.7\overline{)0.050}$ ㉓ $15.5\overline{)6.1}$ ㉔ $15.4\overline{)0.79}$ ㉕ $7.1\overline{)0.78}$

㉖ $2.58\overline{)3.2}$ ㉗ $10.3\overline{)8.05}$ ㉘ $6.2\overline{)0.79}$ ㉙ $33.2\overline{)0.089}$ ㉚ $24.5\overline{)0.16}$

Name: ———————————————— **Date:** ——————

Converting Decimals To Percentages

Time:

:

Score:

/100

Convert.

2 points per question

(1) 0.389 =

(2) 0.56 =

(3) 0.147 =

(4) 0.198 =

(5) 0.45 =

(6) 0.445 =

(7) 0.472 =

(8) 0.435 =

(9) 0.913 =

(10) 0.05 =

(11) 0.688 =

(12) 0.558 =

(13) 0.458 =

(14) 0.665 =

(15) 0.942 =

(16) 0.97 =

(17) 0.212 =

(18) 0.557 =

(19) 0.134 =

(20) 0.48 =

(21) 0.075 =

(22) 0.075 =

(23) 0.895 =

(24) 0.41 =

(25) 0.855 =

Convert.

① $84\frac{1}{4}\% =$

② $1\frac{4}{5}\% =$

③ $18\% =$

④ $31\frac{5}{10}\% =$

⑤ $90\frac{1}{4}\% =$

⑥ $55\frac{2}{5}\% =$

⑦ $51\frac{1}{2}\% =$

⑧ $66\% =$

⑨ $57\frac{3}{5}\% =$

⑩ $74\frac{1}{2}\% =$

⑪ $74\frac{1}{10}\% =$

⑫ $67\frac{1}{4}\% =$

⑬ $93\% =$

⑭ $60\frac{2}{4}\% =$

⑮ $63\frac{3}{5}\% =$

⑯ $70\frac{4}{10}\% =$

⑰ $42\frac{1}{2}\% =$

⑱ $51\frac{1}{4}\% =$

⑲ $49\frac{1}{2}\% =$

⑳ $52\frac{3}{10}\% =$

㉑ $60\frac{1}{5}\% =$

㉒ $6\% =$

㉓ $70\frac{6}{10}\% =$

㉔ $58\% =$

㉕ $47\frac{1}{2}\% =$

36

Name: _____ Date: _____

Converting Decimals To Percentages

Time: **:**

Score: **/100**

Convert.

2 points per question

(1) 0.821 =

(2) 1 =

(3) 0.155 =

(4) 0.477 =

(5) 0.32 =

(6) 0.965 =

(7) 0.099 =

(8) 0.864 =

(9) 0.238 =

(10) 0.04 =

(11) 0.412 =

(12) 0.365 =

(13) 0.393 =

(14) 0.075 =

(15) 0.838 =

(16) 0.734 =

(17) 0.932 =

(18) 0.637 =

(19) 0.408 =

(20) 0.01 =

(21) 0.125 =

(22) 0.895 =

(23) 0.67 =

(24) 0.465 =

(25) 0.303 =

Convert.

(1) $8\frac{4}{5}\% =$

(2) $87\frac{5}{10}\% =$

(3) $41\% =$

(4) $62\frac{4}{10}\% =$

(5) $30\frac{1}{2}\% =$

(6) $72\frac{3}{4}\% =$

(7) $3\frac{1}{3}\% =$

(8) $93\frac{2}{5}\% =$

(9) $81\frac{2}{3}\% =$

(10) $38\frac{1}{5}\% =$

(11) $91\frac{9}{10}\% =$

(12) $92\frac{1}{2}\% =$

(13) $43\frac{2}{4}\% =$

(14) $26\% =$

(15) $44\frac{1}{4}\% =$

(16) $82\frac{1}{2}\% =$

(17) $47\frac{3}{10}\% =$

(18) $78\frac{2}{3}\% =$

(19) $7\% =$

(20) $20\% =$

(21) $75\frac{4}{5}\% =$

(22) $66\frac{4}{10}\% =$

(23) $33\frac{2}{3}\% =$

(24) $53\frac{1}{4}\% =$

(25) $1\frac{1}{2}\% =$

Name: _____ Date: _____

Multiplication Decimals By 0.1, 0.01 and 0.001

Time:

:

Score:

/100

Find the product.

2 points per question

①   4.9
× 0.02

②   0.71
× 0.002

③   2.4
× 0.001

④   6.6
× 0.009

⑤   9.05
× 0.03

⑥   7.4
× 0.08

⑦   0.16
× 0.004

⑧   9.5
× 0.6

⑨   0.70
× 0.2

⑩   7.4
× 0.006

⑪   0.84
× 0.003

⑫   3.2
× 0.4

⑬   0.57
× 0.006

⑭   3.6
× 0.009

⑮   6.7
× 0.04

⑯   0.45
× 0.2

⑰   0.34
× 0.004

⑱   2.4
× 0.02

⑲   8.5
× 0.07

⑳   0.74
× 0.3

Find the product.

1) 0.72
× 0.8

2) 7.0
× 0.1

3) 84
× 0.6

4) 90
× 0.5

5) 63
× 0.005

6) 5.8
× 0.008

7) 1.5
× 0.05

8) 1.07
× 0.02

9) 5.2
× 0.006

10) 8.05
× 0.4

11) 4.6
× 0.3

12) 0.63
× 0.001

13) 8.6
× 0.007

14) 0.65
× 0.2

15) 3.9
× 0.004

16) 0.29
× 0.006

17) 0.21
× 0.8

18) 5.9
× 0.5

19) 9.01
× 0.8

20) 7.7
× 0.8

21) 1.6
× 0.01

22) 0.18
× 0.2

23) 2.7
× 0.09

24) 0.24
× 0.001

25) 0.28
× 0.4

26) 0.25
× 0.07

27) 0.62
× 0.02

28) 7.3
× 0.009

29) 8.7
× 0.2

30) 5.7
× 0.4

Name: _____ Date: _____

Multiplication Decimals By 0.1, 0.01 and 0.001

Time:
:

Score:
/100

Find the product.

2 points per question

(1)
4.1
× 0.01

(2)
9.7
× 0.1

(3)
9.5
× 0.01

(4)
0.73
× 0.01

(5)
0.92
× 0.1

(6)
0.89
× 0.1

(7)
0.87
× 0.001

(8)
0.21
× 0.01

(9)
7.4
× 0.1

(10)
3.5
× 0.001

(11)
9.6
× 0.1

(12)
0.15
× 0.01

(13)
0.81
× 0.01

(14)
6.3
× 0.1

(15)
6.5
× 0.001

(16)
4.8
× 0.01

(17)
0.50
× 0.001

(18)
2.6
× 0.001

(19)
5.7
× 0.01

(20)
1.6
× 0.01

Find the product.

①   1.7
  × 0.001

②   0.42
  × 0.1

③   0.26
  × 0.1

④   5.6
  × 0.001

⑤   4.9
  × 0.1

⑥   1.1
  × 0.001

⑦   0.67
  × 0.01

⑧   2.3
  × 0.01

⑨   0.57
  × 0.01

⑩   5.5
  × 0.01

⑪   2.0
  × 0.1

⑫   2.3
  × 0.001

⑬   0.46
  × 0.01

⑭   5.5
  × 0.1

⑮   0.14
  × 0.01

⑯   0.10
  × 0.01

⑰   2.5
  × 0.1

⑱   2.4
  × 0.001

⑲   0.48
  × 0.01

⑳   10.0
  × 0.1

㉑   2.8
  × 0.1

㉒   0.34
  × 0.001

㉓   1.2
  × 0.01

㉔   0.28
  × 0.1

㉕   7.8
  × 0.01

㉖   6.14
  × 0.001

㉗   1.14
  × 0.001

㉘   5.4
  × 0.001

㉙   8.2
  × 0.1

㉚   0.39
  × 0.1

Name: _____ Date: _____

Multiplication Decimals By 10, 100 and 1000

Time:

:

Score:

/100

Find the product.

2 points per question

①   0.36
   × 1,000

②   6.3
   × 100

③   0.21
   × 1,000

④   9.95
   × 100

⑤   4.32
   × 10

⑥   2.2
   × 10

⑦   0.98
   × 1,000

⑧   0.67
   × 100

⑨   0.40
   × 100

⑩   3.33
   × 10

⑪   7.4
   × 1,000

⑫   7.5
   × 100

⑬   8.9
   × 1,000

⑭   0.75
   × 1,000

⑮   0.22
   × 1,000

⑯   0.62
   × 1,000

⑰   7.4
   × 10

⑱   4.4
   × 10

⑲   0.61
   × 100

⑳   3.6
   × 10

Find the product.

1. 0.47 × 100

2. 0.51 × 1,000

3. 5.6 × 10

4. 2.1 × 10

5. 7.02 × 100

6. 0.65 × 100

7. 0.80 × 1,000

8. 0.96 × 100

9. 8.5 × 10

10. 0.70 × 1,000

11. 1.45 × 10

12. 6.9 × 100

13. 9.401 × 10

14. 0.73 × 100

15. 8.9 × 1,000

16. 5.3 × 10

17. 2.35 × 1,000

18. 1.15 × 10

19. 4.9 × 10

20. 1.3 × 1,000

21. 9.5 × 100

22. 8.8 × 1,000

23. 0.50 × 100

24. 1.6 × 10

25. 0.44 × 10

26. 0.73 × 1,000

27. 7.9 × 1,000

28. 0.13 × 1,000

29. 4.7 × 1,000

30. 9.02 × 100

Name: ——————————— Date: ————

Multiplication Decimals By 10, 100 and 1000

Time:

:

Score:

/100

Find the product.

2 points per question

①   0.45
   × 1,000
—————

②   4.4
   × 100
—————

③   1.07
   × 10
—————

④   5.2
   × 100
—————

⑤   7.1
   × 10
—————

⑥   0.61
   × 10
—————

⑦   7.3
   × 100
—————

⑧   0.33
   × 10
—————

⑨   0.31
   × 100
—————

⑩   0.59
   × 1,000
—————

⑪   0.54
   × 1,000
—————

⑫   9.1
   × 100
—————

⑬   0.51
   × 1,000
—————

⑭   0.75
   × 1,000
—————

⑮   6.9
   × 1,000
—————

⑯   0.70
   × 100
—————

⑰   2.7
   × 10
—————

⑱   0.41
   × 10
—————

⑲   0.115
   × 100
—————

⑳   4.6
   × 1,000
—————

Find the product.

1. 0.60 × 10

2. 4.7 × 100

3. 0.78 × 1,000

4. 0.65 × 100

5. 0.27 × 100

6. 4.0 × 10

7. 0.45 × 10

8. 9.2 × 1,000

9. 6.4 × 1,000

10. 3.5 × 1,000

11. 3.5 × 10

12. 0.93 × 10

13. 0.93 × 100

14. 0.15 × 1,000

15. 9.0 × 1,000

16. 0.21 × 100

17. 0.22 × 100

18. 0.79 × 1,000

19. 6.8 × 100

20. 0.81 × 10

21. 10.11 × 100

22. 8.9 × 10

23. 25.3 × 100

24. 6.72 × 10

25. 3.9 × 10

26. 1.4 × 100

27. 48.5 × 1,000

28. 56.7 × 1,000

29. 7.89 × 10

30. 7.2 × 1,000

Name: ———————————— Date: ————————

Fractions on Number Lines

Time:

:

Score:

/100

Identify where each fraction should be placed on the number lines below.   5 points per question

(1) $\frac{1}{10}$ $1\frac{1}{10}$ $1\frac{2}{5}$ $\frac{2}{5}$ $\frac{4}{5}$

0   2

(2) $\frac{5}{8}$ $1\frac{1}{2}$ $\frac{1}{4}$ $1\frac{1}{8}$ $1\frac{7}{8}$

0   2

(3) $1\frac{9}{10}$ $1\frac{1}{2}$ $\frac{3}{10}$ $1\frac{1}{5}$ $\frac{9}{10}$

0   2

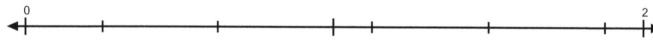

(4) $\frac{1}{8}$ $1\frac{1}{4}$ $1\frac{7}{8}$ $\frac{1}{2}$ $\frac{7}{8}$

0   2

(5) $\frac{3}{8}$ $1\frac{1}{8}$ $\frac{3}{4}$ $1\frac{3}{4}$ $1\frac{1}{2}$

0   2

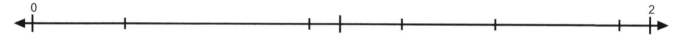

(6) $\frac{3}{10}$ $1\frac{9}{10}$ 1 $\frac{7}{10}$ $1\frac{3}{5}$

0   2

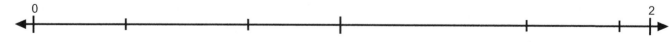

(7) $\dfrac{1}{2}$ $\dfrac{1}{5}$ $1\dfrac{3}{10}$ 1 $1\dfrac{9}{10}$

0   2

(8) $\dfrac{1}{8}$ $\dfrac{3}{8}$ $1\dfrac{3}{4}$ $1\dfrac{1}{4}$ $\dfrac{5}{8}$

0   2

(9) $1\dfrac{4}{5}$ $\dfrac{3}{5}$ $\dfrac{1}{5}$ $\dfrac{9}{10}$ $1\dfrac{2}{5}$

0   2

(10) $1\dfrac{7}{8}$ $\dfrac{7}{8}$ $1\dfrac{1}{2}$ $\dfrac{1}{8}$ $\dfrac{1}{2}$

0   2

(11) $\dfrac{9}{10}$ $1\dfrac{3}{10}$ $\dfrac{1}{10}$ $\dfrac{1}{2}$ $1\dfrac{3}{5}$

0   2

(12) 1 $1\dfrac{1}{2}$ $1\dfrac{7}{8}$ $1\dfrac{1}{4}$ $\dfrac{1}{4}$

0   2

(13) $1\dfrac{7}{8}$ $1\dfrac{1}{2}$ $\dfrac{5}{8}$ 1 $\dfrac{1}{4}$

0   2

(14) $\frac{2}{5}$ $\frac{1}{10}$ 1 $1\frac{1}{2}$ $1\frac{9}{10}$

0 ———————————————————————————— 2

(15) $1\frac{1}{2}$ $1\frac{1}{8}$ $\frac{3}{4}$ $\frac{3}{8}$ $1\frac{7}{8}$

0 ———————————————————————————— 2

(16) $1\frac{4}{5}$ $\frac{9}{10}$ $\frac{1}{5}$ $1\frac{1}{2}$ $\frac{3}{5}$

0 ———————————————————————————— 2

(17) $\frac{1}{5}$ $1\frac{3}{5}$ $\frac{9}{10}$ $1\frac{3}{10}$ $\frac{1}{2}$

0 ———————————————————————————— 2

(18) $1\frac{3}{4}$ $1\frac{1}{2}$ $\frac{1}{4}$ $1\frac{1}{4}$ $\frac{7}{8}$

0 ———————————————————————————— 2

(19) $\frac{3}{4}$ $\frac{3}{8}$ $1\frac{7}{8}$ $1\frac{1}{2}$ $1\frac{1}{8}$

0 ———————————————————————————— 2

(20) $\frac{4}{5}$ $1\frac{4}{5}$ $1\frac{3}{10}$ $\frac{1}{10}$ $\frac{1}{2}$

0 ———————————————————————————— 2

Name: _____ Date: _____

Time:
:

Score:
/100

Decimals on Number Lines

Identify where each decimal should be placed on the number lines below.   5 points per question

① 0.3   1.8   1   1.4   0.8

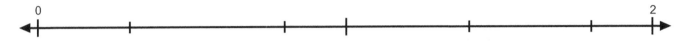

② 0.8   0.2   0.4   1.9   1.1

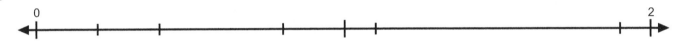

③ 1.1   0.7   0.4   0.1   1.9

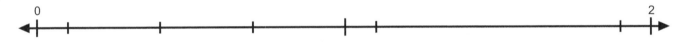

④ 0.1   1   1.7   0.8   0.6

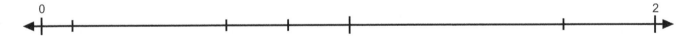

⑤ 1   0.3   1.8   1.5   0.8

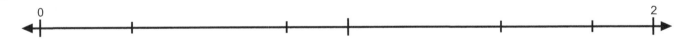

⑥ 0.8   1.5   0.6   1.8   1

(7) **0.3   0.5   1.1   1.9   1.4**

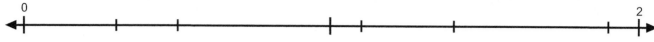

(8) **0.3   1.1   1.6   0.8   0.5**

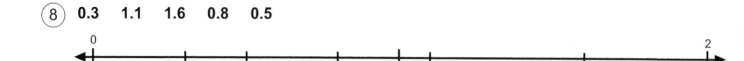

(9) **0.6   1.4   0.1   1.6   0.8**

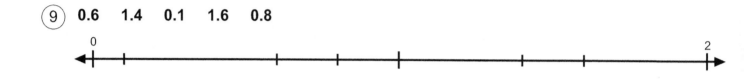

(10) **0.7   1.9   1.7   0.1   1**

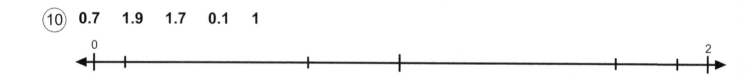

(11) **1.4   1.8   1.2   0.8   0.5**

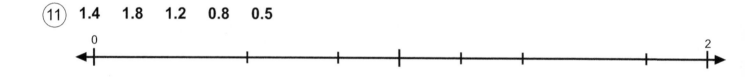

(12) **0.2   1.2   1.7   1.9   0.6**

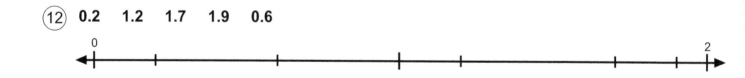

(13) **0.7   0.3   1.8   0.1   0.9**

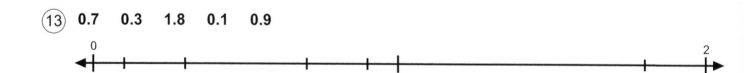

14) **1.4   1.9   1   0.5   0.7**

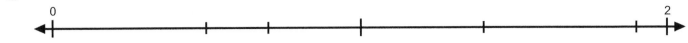

15) **0.9   0.1   0.3   1.4   0.6**

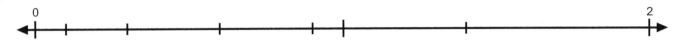

16) **0.7   0.2   1.9   1.3   1.5**

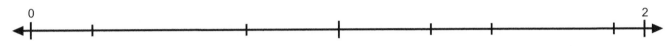

17) **1.9   1.7   1.2   0.2   0.5**

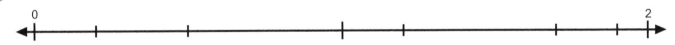

18) **1.4   1.2   1.6   1.9   1**

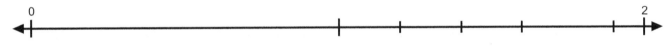

19) **1.8   0.1   0.8   1.1   0.4**

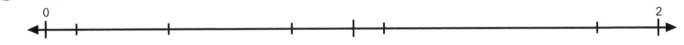

20) **1.8   1.4   0.8   0.4   1**

Page 1

1) $\frac{3}{8} > \frac{1}{4}$ 2) $\frac{5}{9} < \frac{2}{3}$ 3) $\frac{3}{6} < \frac{3}{5}$ 4) $\frac{8}{9} > \frac{2}{8}$ 5) $\frac{3}{4} > \frac{3}{6}$ 6) $\frac{2}{5} < \frac{2}{3}$ 7) $\frac{2}{6} = \frac{3}{9}$

8) $\frac{4}{5} > \frac{2}{8}$ 9) $\frac{2}{4} < \frac{2}{3}$ 10) $\frac{2}{4} < \frac{6}{8}$ 11) $\frac{2}{3} > \frac{1}{5}$ 12) $\frac{1}{9} < \frac{1}{6}$ 13) $\frac{3}{4} > \frac{1}{6}$ 14) $\frac{3}{5} < \frac{6}{9}$

15) $\frac{4}{8} < \frac{2}{3}$ 16) $\frac{2}{4} > \frac{2}{6}$ 17) $\frac{3}{9} < \frac{7}{8}$ 18) $\frac{1}{3} < \frac{4}{5}$ 19) $\frac{3}{5} > \frac{2}{4}$ 20) $\frac{6}{8} > \frac{1}{9}$

Page 2

1) $\frac{2}{8} < \frac{2}{7}$ 2) $\frac{2}{5} > \frac{1}{4}$ 3) $\frac{1}{7} < \frac{2}{10}$ 4) $\frac{7}{8} > \frac{4}{6}$ 5) $\frac{2}{3} < \frac{4}{5}$ 6) $\frac{4}{9} < \frac{5}{7}$ 7) $\frac{7}{9} > \frac{1}{6}$

8) $\frac{5}{10} < \frac{2}{3}$ 9) $\frac{2}{5} < \frac{4}{8}$ 10) $\frac{2}{4} < \frac{2}{3}$ 11) $\frac{3}{7} > \frac{1}{4}$ 12) $\frac{3}{6} > \frac{1}{5}$ 13) $\frac{8}{10} > \frac{3}{8}$ 14) $\frac{4}{9} < \frac{6}{10}$

15) $\frac{2}{5} < \frac{7}{8}$ 16) $\frac{2}{4} > \frac{2}{9}$ 17) $\frac{1}{3} < \frac{5}{6}$ 18) $\frac{2}{7} > \frac{1}{8}$ 19) $\frac{5}{6} > \frac{4}{7}$ 20) $\frac{7}{9} > \frac{6}{10}$ 21) $\frac{3}{4} > \frac{2}{6}$

22) $\frac{4}{5} < \frac{7}{8}$ 23) $\frac{1}{9} < \frac{2}{7}$ 24) $\frac{1}{3} > \frac{3}{10}$ 25) $\frac{1}{4} < \frac{2}{3}$ 26) $\frac{6}{10} > \frac{3}{9}$ 27) $\frac{5}{7} > \frac{1}{8}$ 28) $\frac{3}{5} > \frac{2}{6}$

29) $\frac{2}{4} < \frac{3}{5}$ 30) $\frac{3}{4} > \frac{3}{10}$

Page 3

1) $\frac{6}{8} > \frac{3}{5}$ 2) $\frac{3}{4} > \frac{1}{3}$ 3) $\frac{4}{6} > \frac{3}{8}$ 4) $\frac{5}{6} > \frac{1}{3}$ 5) $\frac{3}{4} < \frac{4}{5}$ 6) $\frac{5}{8} > \frac{2}{6}$ 7) $\frac{1}{5} < \frac{2}{4}$

8) $\frac{2}{3} < \frac{4}{5}$ 9) $\frac{1}{3} > \frac{1}{4}$ 10) $\frac{2}{8} < \frac{2}{6}$ 11) $\frac{2}{3} > \frac{4}{8}$ 12) $\frac{1}{4} > \frac{1}{5}$ 13) $\frac{3}{6} < \frac{7}{8}$ 14) $\frac{3}{5} < \frac{2}{3}$

15) $\frac{1}{4} < \frac{5}{6}$ 16) $\frac{5}{6} > \frac{3}{5}$ 17) $\frac{2}{4} = \frac{4}{8}$ 18) $\frac{1}{3} > \frac{2}{8}$ 19) $\frac{4}{5} > \frac{3}{6}$ 20) $\frac{3}{4} > \frac{2}{3}$

Page 4

1) $\frac{2}{3} > \frac{2}{7}$ 2) $\frac{4}{5} > \frac{3}{4}$ 3) $\frac{2}{6} > \frac{2}{8}$ 4) $\frac{7}{10} > \frac{1}{3}$ 5) $\frac{1}{9} < \frac{3}{4}$ 6) $\frac{1}{10} < \frac{3}{8}$ 7) $\frac{4}{7} < \frac{5}{6}$

8) $\frac{2}{3} = \frac{6}{9}$ 9) $\frac{2}{5} > \frac{3}{9}$ 10) $\frac{2}{3} = \frac{4}{6}$ 11) $\frac{2}{8} < \frac{2}{7}$ 12) $\frac{2}{10} < \frac{2}{4}$ 13) $\frac{2}{5} = \frac{2}{5}$ 14) $\frac{2}{7} < \frac{1}{3}$

15) $\frac{4}{8} < \frac{3}{4}$ 16) $\frac{1}{9} < \frac{6}{10}$ 17) $\frac{1}{6} < \frac{3}{4}$ 18) $\frac{2}{3} > \frac{3}{5}$ 19) $\frac{1}{6} < \frac{2}{9}$ 20) $\frac{3}{10} < \frac{4}{8}$ 21) $\frac{5}{7} < \frac{3}{4}$

22) $\frac{2}{5} > \frac{1}{3}$ 23) $\frac{3}{6} > \frac{1}{7}$ 24) $\frac{7}{10} < \frac{8}{9}$ 25) $\frac{7}{8} > \frac{1}{3}$ 26) $\frac{6}{10} < \frac{3}{4}$ 27) $\frac{2}{7} < \frac{4}{5}$ 28) $\frac{2}{9} < \frac{4}{8}$

29) $\frac{1}{6} < \frac{1}{3}$ 30) $\frac{3}{6} < \frac{3}{4}$

Page 5

1) $\frac{21}{28} = \frac{3}{4}$ 2) $\frac{4}{8} = \frac{1}{2}$ 3) $\frac{7}{21} = \frac{1}{3}$ 4) $\frac{18}{54} = \frac{1}{3}$ 5) $\frac{27}{45} = \frac{3}{5}$ 6) $\frac{32}{80} = \frac{2}{5}$ 7) $\frac{6}{12} = \frac{1}{2}$

8) $\frac{2}{20} = \frac{1}{10}$ 9) $\frac{6}{18} = \frac{1}{3}$ 10) $\frac{56}{72} = \frac{7}{9}$ 11) $\frac{27}{72} = \frac{3}{8}$ 12) $\frac{3}{12} = \frac{1}{4}$ 13) $\frac{25}{30} = \frac{5}{6}$ 14) $\frac{3}{15} = \frac{1}{5}$

15) $\frac{40}{64} = \frac{5}{8}$ 16) $\frac{14}{21} = \frac{2}{3}$ 17) $\frac{5}{10} = \frac{1}{2}$ 18) $\frac{2}{12} = \frac{1}{6}$ 19) $\frac{6}{20} = \frac{3}{10}$ 20) $\frac{18}{36} = \frac{1}{2}$

Page 6

1) $\frac{18}{30} = \frac{3}{5}$ 2) $\frac{10}{12} = \frac{5}{6}$ 3) $\frac{4}{12} = \frac{1}{3}$ 4) $\frac{49}{63} = \frac{7}{9}$ 5) $\frac{10}{20} = \frac{1}{2}$ 6) $\frac{16}{80} = \frac{1}{5}$ 7) $\frac{8}{12} = \frac{2}{3}$

8) $\frac{8}{64} = \frac{1}{8}$ 9) $\frac{9}{15} = \frac{3}{5}$ 10) $\frac{6}{12} = \frac{1}{2}$ 11) $\frac{6}{8} = \frac{3}{4}$ 12) $\frac{3}{6} = \frac{1}{2}$ 13) $\frac{3}{27} = \frac{1}{9}$ 14) $\frac{2}{12} = \frac{1}{6}$

15) $\frac{5}{25} = \frac{1}{5}$ 16) $\frac{18}{60} = \frac{3}{10}$ 17) $\frac{35}{45} = \frac{7}{9}$ 18) $\frac{8}{24} = \frac{1}{3}$ 19) $\frac{20}{32} = \frac{5}{8}$ 20) $\frac{16}{20} = \frac{4}{5}$ 21) $\frac{40}{48} = \frac{5}{6}$

22) $\frac{4}{16} = \frac{1}{4}$ 23) $\frac{6}{18} = \frac{1}{3}$ 24) $\frac{42}{56} = \frac{3}{4}$ 25) $\frac{9}{81} = \frac{1}{9}$ 26) $\frac{15}{20} = \frac{3}{4}$ 27) $\frac{18}{24} = \frac{3}{4}$ 28) $\frac{12}{18} = \frac{2}{3}$

29) $\frac{10}{50} = \frac{1}{5}$ 30) $\frac{12}{30} = \frac{2}{5}$

Page 7

(1) $\frac{18}{36} = \frac{1}{2}$ (2) $\frac{6}{18} = \frac{1}{3}$ (3) $\frac{4}{8} = \frac{1}{2}$ (4) $\frac{12}{24} = \frac{1}{2}$ (5) $\frac{15}{25} = \frac{3}{5}$ (6) $\frac{4}{12} = \frac{1}{3}$ (7) $\frac{6}{12} = \frac{1}{2}$

(8) $\frac{4}{16} = \frac{1}{4}$ (9) $\frac{9}{27} = \frac{1}{3}$ (10) $\frac{25}{30} = \frac{5}{6}$ (11) $\frac{30}{40} = \frac{3}{4}$ (12) $\frac{18}{60} = \frac{3}{10}$ (13) $\frac{9}{45} = \frac{1}{5}$ (14) $\frac{28}{40} = \frac{7}{10}$

(15) $\frac{9}{18} = \frac{1}{2}$ (16) $\frac{72}{81} = \frac{8}{9}$ (17) $\frac{15}{30} = \frac{1}{2}$ (18) $\frac{35}{56} = \frac{5}{8}$ (19) $\frac{14}{21} = \frac{2}{3}$ (20) $\frac{8}{64} = \frac{1}{8}$

Page 8

(1) $\frac{10}{30} = \frac{1}{3}$ (2) $\frac{4}{8} = \frac{1}{2}$ (3) $\frac{4}{12} = \frac{1}{3}$ (4) $\frac{3}{18} = \frac{1}{6}$ (5) $\frac{30}{45} = \frac{2}{3}$ (6) $\frac{12}{16} = \frac{3}{4}$ (7) $\frac{81}{90} = \frac{9}{10}$

(8) $\frac{27}{36} = \frac{3}{4}$ (9) $\frac{6}{12} = \frac{1}{2}$ (10) $\frac{16}{20} = \frac{4}{5}$ (11) $\frac{40}{45} = \frac{8}{9}$ (12) $\frac{9}{18} = \frac{1}{2}$ (13) $\frac{30}{40} = \frac{3}{4}$ (14) $\frac{6}{36} = \frac{1}{6}$

(15) $\frac{28}{35} = \frac{4}{5}$ (16) $\frac{9}{30} = \frac{3}{10}$ (17) $\frac{2}{8} = \frac{1}{4}$ (18) $\frac{24}{30} = \frac{4}{5}$ (19) $\frac{20}{50} = \frac{2}{5}$ (20) $\frac{7}{28} = \frac{1}{4}$ (21) $\frac{3}{6} = \frac{1}{2}$

(22) $\frac{30}{54} = \frac{5}{9}$ (23) $\frac{6}{18} = \frac{1}{3}$ (24) $\frac{40}{64} = \frac{5}{8}$ (25) $\frac{12}{24} = \frac{1}{2}$ (26) $\frac{21}{56} = \frac{3}{8}$ (27) $\frac{63}{81} = \frac{7}{9}$ (28) $\frac{8}{16} = \frac{1}{2}$

(29) $\frac{16}{24} = \frac{2}{3}$ (30) $\frac{21}{42} = \frac{1}{2}$

Page 9

(1) $\frac{4}{6} = \frac{28}{42}$ (2) $\frac{1}{2} = \frac{7}{14}$ (3) $\frac{5}{8} = \frac{40}{64}$ (4) $\frac{3}{4} = \frac{18}{24}$ (5) $\frac{2}{3} = \frac{14}{21}$ (6) $\frac{5}{9} = \frac{45}{81}$ (7) $\frac{3}{5} = \frac{12}{20}$

(8) $\frac{1}{3} = \frac{4}{12}$ (9) $\frac{4}{7} = \frac{20}{35}$ (10) $\frac{6}{9} = \frac{24}{36}$ (11) $\frac{2}{6} = \frac{4}{12}$ (12) $\frac{1}{5} = \frac{4}{20}$ (13) $\frac{3}{4} = \frac{9}{12}$ (14) $\frac{2}{8} = \frac{16}{64}$

(15) $\frac{1}{2} = \frac{8}{16}$ (16) $\frac{1}{2} = \frac{4}{8}$ (17) $\frac{1}{4} = \frac{2}{8}$ (18) $\frac{5}{8} = \frac{25}{40}$ (19) $\frac{2}{3} = \frac{8}{12}$ (20) $\frac{3}{6} = \frac{9}{18}$

Page 10

(1) $\frac{5}{6} = \frac{25}{30}$ (2) $\frac{1}{4} = \frac{2}{8}$ (3) $\frac{2}{4} = \frac{12}{24}$ (4) $\frac{1}{6} = \frac{4}{24}$ (5) $\frac{5}{8} = \frac{20}{32}$ (6) $\frac{2}{3} = \frac{16}{24}$ (7) $\frac{2}{5} = \frac{20}{50}$

(8) $\frac{3}{6} = \frac{24}{48}$ (9) $\frac{7}{8} = \frac{28}{32}$ (10) $\frac{3}{4} = \frac{21}{28}$ (11) $\frac{1}{5} = \frac{4}{20}$ (12) $\frac{2}{3} = \frac{4}{6}$ (13) $\frac{4}{6} = \frac{32}{48}$ (14) $\frac{3}{5} = \frac{21}{35}$

(15) $\frac{1}{8} = \frac{8}{64}$ (16) $\frac{2}{3} = \frac{14}{21}$ (17) $\frac{1}{4} = \frac{3}{12}$ (18) $\frac{2}{6} = \frac{8}{24}$ (19) $\frac{1}{3} = \frac{9}{27}$ (20) $\frac{1}{8} = \frac{4}{32}$ (21) $\frac{1}{5} = \frac{6}{30}$

(22) $\frac{4}{6} = \frac{36}{54}$ (23) $\frac{4}{8} = \frac{36}{72}$ (24) $\frac{2}{3} = \frac{10}{15}$ (25) $\frac{2}{4} = \frac{18}{36}$ (26) $\frac{2}{5} = \frac{18}{45}$ (27) $\frac{4}{8} = \frac{16}{32}$ (28) $\frac{4}{6} = \frac{40}{60}$

(29) $\frac{2}{3} = \frac{8}{12}$ (30) $\frac{2}{4} = \frac{8}{16}$

Page 11

(1) $\frac{3}{4} = \frac{18}{24}$ (2) $\frac{1}{8} = \frac{7}{56}$ (3) $\frac{3}{4} = \frac{12}{16}$ (4) $\frac{4}{5} = \frac{8}{10}$ (5) $\frac{4}{6} = \frac{32}{48}$ (6) $\frac{1}{3} = \frac{2}{6}$ (7) $\frac{4}{8} = \frac{28}{56}$

(8) $\frac{1}{4} = \frac{9}{36}$ (9) $\frac{1}{6} = \frac{3}{18}$ (10) $\frac{2}{3} = \frac{16}{24}$ (11) $\frac{2}{5} = \frac{20}{50}$ (12) $\frac{1}{8} = \frac{4}{32}$ (13) $\frac{1}{6} = \frac{4}{24}$ (14) $\frac{2}{4} = \frac{14}{28}$

(15) $\frac{2}{3} = \frac{4}{6}$ (16) $\frac{4}{6} = \frac{8}{12}$ (17) $\frac{1}{3} = \frac{9}{27}$ (18) $\frac{7}{8} = \frac{42}{48}$ (19) $\frac{4}{5} = \frac{20}{25}$ (20) $\frac{1}{4} = \frac{8}{32}$

Page 12

(1) $\frac{3}{4} = \frac{15}{20}$ (2) $\frac{4}{6} = \frac{40}{60}$ (3) $\frac{1}{3} = \frac{9}{27}$ (4) $\frac{1}{5} = \frac{5}{25}$ (5) $\frac{5}{8} = \frac{25}{40}$ (6) $\frac{2}{3} = \frac{12}{18}$ (7) $\frac{2}{8} = \frac{14}{56}$

(8) $\frac{3}{6} = \frac{18}{36}$ (9) $\frac{3}{4} = \frac{21}{28}$ (10) $\frac{2}{8} = \frac{8}{32}$ (11) $\frac{4}{5} = \frac{16}{20}$ (12) $\frac{3}{4} = \frac{27}{36}$ (13) $\frac{1}{3} = \frac{8}{24}$ (14) $\frac{1}{6} = \frac{7}{42}$

(15) $\frac{2}{4} = \frac{10}{20}$ (16) $\frac{1}{3} = \frac{7}{21}$ (17) $\frac{3}{8} = \frac{27}{72}$ (18) $\frac{1}{4} = \frac{4}{16}$ (19) $\frac{4}{6} = \frac{20}{30}$ (20) $\frac{6}{8} = \frac{60}{80}$ (21) $\frac{3}{5} = \frac{21}{35}$

(22) $\frac{4}{8} = \frac{28}{56}$ (23) $\frac{2}{6} = \frac{12}{36}$ (24) $\frac{3}{5} = \frac{24}{40}$ (25) $\frac{1}{3} = \frac{4}{12}$ (26) $\frac{5}{6} = \frac{10}{12}$ (27) $\frac{4}{5} = \frac{32}{40}$ (28) $\frac{1}{4} = \frac{3}{12}$

(29) $\frac{7}{8} = \frac{49}{56}$ (30) $\frac{1}{3} = \frac{6}{18}$

Page 13

1) $\frac{3}{9} + \frac{5}{6} = \frac{7}{6}$
2) $\frac{1}{9} + \frac{2}{10} = \frac{14}{45}$
3) $\frac{3}{6} + \frac{1}{2} = \frac{1}{1}$
4) $\frac{5}{7} + \frac{3}{4} = \frac{41}{28}$
5) $\frac{1}{8} + \frac{2}{3} = \frac{19}{24}$
6) $\frac{2}{5} + \frac{1}{11} = \frac{27}{55}$
7) $\frac{5}{7} + \frac{1}{6} = \frac{37}{42}$
8) $\frac{1}{3} + \frac{2}{4} = \frac{5}{6}$
9) $\frac{8}{9} + \frac{2}{9} = \frac{10}{9}$
10) $\frac{5}{9} + \frac{1}{6} = \frac{13}{18}$
11) $\frac{1}{6} + \frac{11}{12} = \frac{13}{12}$
12) $\frac{3}{4} + \frac{1}{5} = \frac{19}{20}$
13) $\frac{2}{3} + \frac{5}{9} = \frac{11}{9}$
14) $\frac{2}{3} + \frac{6}{12} = \frac{7}{6}$
15) $\frac{3}{6} + \frac{8}{10} = \frac{13}{10}$
16) $\frac{1}{2} + \frac{3}{6} = \frac{1}{1}$
17) $\frac{5}{8} + \frac{1}{2} = \frac{9}{8}$
18) $\frac{1}{3} + \frac{1}{3} = \frac{2}{3}$
19) $\frac{5}{8} + \frac{4}{5} = \frac{57}{40}$
20) $\frac{4}{5} + \frac{1}{4} = \frac{21}{20}$

Page 14

1) $\frac{1}{3} + \frac{3}{5} = \frac{14}{15}$
2) $\frac{6}{11} + \frac{1}{2} = \frac{23}{22}$
3) $\frac{2}{6} + \frac{2}{12} = \frac{1}{2}$
4) $\frac{8}{12} + \frac{3}{4} = \frac{17}{12}$
5) $\frac{5}{9} + \frac{3}{6} = \frac{19}{18}$
6) $\frac{2}{3} + \frac{5}{6} = \frac{3}{2}$
7) $\frac{2}{5} + \frac{3}{12} = \frac{13}{20}$
8) $\frac{2}{12} + \frac{1}{11} = \frac{17}{66}$
9) $\frac{3}{4} + \frac{4}{5} = \frac{31}{20}$
10) $\frac{8}{9} + \frac{1}{9} = \frac{1}{1}$
11) $\frac{5}{10} + \frac{3}{4} = \frac{5}{4}$
12) $\frac{2}{6} + \frac{8}{12} = \frac{1}{1}$
13) $\frac{3}{9} + \frac{1}{3} = \frac{2}{3}$
14) $\frac{1}{3} + \frac{1}{2} = \frac{5}{6}$
15) $\frac{6}{8} + \frac{2}{8} = \frac{1}{1}$
16) $\frac{1}{2} + \frac{1}{3} = \frac{5}{6}$
17) $\frac{4}{9} + \frac{8}{10} = \frac{56}{45}$
18) $\frac{3}{4} + \frac{1}{4} = \frac{1}{1}$
19) $\frac{7}{8} + \frac{2}{6} = \frac{29}{24}$
20) $\frac{1}{3} + \frac{2}{12} = \frac{1}{2}$
21) $\frac{6}{11} + \frac{3}{8} = \frac{81}{88}$
22) $\frac{1}{5} + \frac{3}{4} = \frac{19}{20}$
23) $\frac{3}{6} + \frac{1}{2} = \frac{1}{1}$
24) $\frac{6}{8} + \frac{4}{6} = \frac{17}{12}$
25) $\frac{1}{9} + \frac{4}{9} = \frac{5}{9}$
26) $\frac{1}{10} + \frac{1}{2} = \frac{3}{5}$
27) $\frac{3}{8} + \frac{2}{12} = \frac{13}{24}$
28) $\frac{7}{10} + \frac{4}{9} = \frac{103}{90}$
29) $\frac{1}{3} + \frac{8}{10} = \frac{17}{15}$
30) $\frac{7}{12} + \frac{1}{6} = \frac{3}{4}$

Page 15

1) $\frac{2}{3} + \frac{1}{3} = \frac{1}{1}$
2) $\frac{1}{8} + \frac{2}{5} = \frac{21}{40}$
3) $\frac{2}{9} + \frac{3}{6} = \frac{13}{18}$
4) $\frac{5}{6} + \frac{2}{3} = \frac{3}{2}$
5) $\frac{1}{3} + \frac{4}{6} = \frac{1}{1}$
6) $\frac{2}{7} + \frac{4}{6} = \frac{20}{21}$
7) $\frac{1}{3} + \frac{1}{4} = \frac{7}{12}$
8) $\frac{4}{6} + \frac{5}{8} = \frac{31}{24}$
9) $\frac{8}{10} + \frac{2}{3} = \frac{22}{15}$
10) $\frac{2}{4} + \frac{1}{4} = \frac{3}{4}$
11) $\frac{1}{2} + \frac{1}{6} = \frac{2}{3}$
12) $\frac{1}{2} + \frac{2}{4} = \frac{1}{1}$
13) $\frac{5}{6} + \frac{1}{8} = \frac{23}{24}$
14) $\frac{2}{3} + \frac{3}{8} = \frac{25}{24}$
15) $\frac{1}{11} + \frac{4}{6} = \frac{25}{33}$
16) $\frac{7}{9} + \frac{1}{4} = \frac{37}{36}$
17) $\frac{4}{10} + \frac{1}{8} = \frac{21}{40}$
18) $\frac{1}{4} + \frac{4}{5} = \frac{21}{20}$
19) $\frac{3}{9} + \frac{4}{6} = \frac{1}{1}$
20) $\frac{4}{7} + \frac{1}{6} = \frac{31}{42}$

Page 16

1) $\frac{4}{6} + \frac{1}{3} = \frac{1}{1}$
2) $\frac{1}{14} + \frac{3}{6} = \frac{4}{7}$
3) $\frac{2}{9} + \frac{3}{6} = \frac{13}{18}$
4) $\frac{4}{5} + \frac{2}{3} = \frac{22}{15}$
5) $\frac{6}{16} + \frac{2}{3} = \frac{25}{24}$
6) $\frac{3}{10} + \frac{6}{8} = \frac{21}{20}$
7) $\frac{1}{3} + \frac{1}{5} = \frac{8}{15}$
8) $\frac{1}{2} + \frac{3}{5} = \frac{11}{10}$
9) $\frac{11}{14} + \frac{3}{4} = \frac{43}{28}$
10) $\frac{5}{11} + \frac{1}{8} = \frac{51}{88}$
11) $\frac{2}{12} + \frac{1}{3} = \frac{1}{2}$
12) $\frac{2}{5} + \frac{2}{5} = \frac{4}{5}$
13) $\frac{2}{3} + \frac{1}{4} = \frac{11}{12}$
14) $\frac{13}{14} + \frac{2}{6} = \frac{53}{42}$
15) $\frac{1}{10} + \frac{3}{5} = \frac{7}{10}$
16) $\frac{8}{11} + \frac{1}{6} = \frac{59}{66}$
17) $\frac{2}{5} + \frac{1}{3} = \frac{11}{15}$
18) $\frac{7}{8} + \frac{1}{3} = \frac{29}{24}$
19) $\frac{1}{12} + \frac{4}{5} = \frac{53}{60}$
20) $\frac{3}{11} + \frac{2}{3} = \frac{31}{33}$
21) $\frac{1}{2} + \frac{1}{5} = \frac{7}{10}$
22) $\frac{2}{6} + \frac{4}{6} = \frac{1}{1}$
23) $\frac{2}{12} + \frac{4}{6} = \frac{5}{6}$
24) $\frac{7}{14} + \frac{1}{5} = \frac{7}{10}$
25) $\frac{1}{5} + \frac{1}{6} = \frac{11}{30}$
26) $\frac{2}{5} + \frac{1}{8} = \frac{21}{40}$
27) $\frac{3}{6} + \frac{2}{4} = \frac{1}{1}$
28) $\frac{11}{16} + \frac{2}{3} = \frac{65}{48}$
29) $\frac{8}{14} + \frac{3}{5} = \frac{41}{35}$
30) $\frac{2}{3} + \frac{2}{8} = \frac{11}{12}$

Page 17

1) $\frac{1}{2} - \frac{2}{6} = \frac{1}{6}$
2) $\frac{6}{8} - \frac{3}{8} = \frac{3}{8}$
3) $\frac{3}{4} - \frac{2}{12} = \frac{7}{12}$
4) $\frac{5}{8} - \frac{2}{6} = \frac{7}{24}$
5) $\frac{4}{5} - \frac{2}{4} = \frac{3}{10}$
6) $\frac{5}{6} - \frac{3}{6} = \frac{1}{3}$
7) $\frac{5}{9} - \frac{1}{3} = \frac{2}{9}$
8) $\frac{4}{6} - \frac{5}{12} = \frac{1}{4}$
9) $\frac{6}{8} - \frac{2}{3} = \frac{1}{12}$
10) $\frac{7}{10} - \frac{1}{5} = \frac{1}{2}$
11) $\frac{2}{5} - \frac{2}{6} = \frac{1}{15}$
12) $\frac{1}{2} - \frac{5}{12} = \frac{1}{12}$
13) $\frac{2}{9} - \frac{1}{5} = \frac{1}{45}$
14) $\frac{7}{8} - \frac{2}{4} = \frac{3}{8}$
15) $\frac{2}{4} - \frac{3}{12} = \frac{1}{4}$
16) $\frac{3}{4} - \frac{1}{6} = \frac{7}{12}$
17) $\frac{6}{9} - \frac{2}{5} = \frac{4}{15}$
18) $\frac{3}{5} - \frac{1}{3} = \frac{4}{15}$
19) $\frac{2}{4} - \frac{1}{3} = \frac{1}{6}$
20) $\frac{2}{8} - \frac{1}{6} = \frac{1}{12}$

Page 18

1) $\frac{1}{2} - \frac{3}{8} = \frac{1}{8}$
2) $\frac{3}{5} - \frac{2}{4} = \frac{1}{10}$
3) $\frac{5}{8} - \frac{1}{3} = \frac{7}{24}$
4) $\frac{5}{10} - \frac{2}{8} = \frac{1}{4}$
5) $\frac{3}{4} - \frac{1}{3} = \frac{5}{12}$
6) $\frac{8}{10} - \frac{2}{3} = \frac{2}{15}$
7) $\frac{3}{4} - \frac{1}{5} = \frac{11}{20}$
8) $\frac{5}{6} - \frac{3}{4} = \frac{1}{12}$
9) $\frac{11}{12} - \frac{1}{5} = \frac{43}{60}$
10) $\frac{7}{8} - \frac{1}{4} = \frac{5}{8}$
11) $\frac{2}{4} - \frac{1}{6} = \frac{1}{3}$
12) $\frac{6}{8} - \frac{2}{3} = \frac{1}{12}$
13) $\frac{7}{12} - \frac{2}{5} = \frac{11}{60}$
14) $\frac{6}{9} - \frac{2}{4} = \frac{1}{6}$
15) $\frac{3}{8} - \frac{1}{8} = \frac{1}{4}$
16) $\frac{1}{2} - \frac{1}{5} = \frac{3}{10}$
17) $\frac{4}{9} - \frac{1}{3} = \frac{1}{9}$
18) $\frac{2}{9} - \frac{1}{6} = \frac{1}{18}$
19) $\frac{3}{4} - \frac{2}{3} = \frac{1}{12}$
20) $\frac{7}{10} - \frac{1}{5} = \frac{1}{2}$
21) $\frac{4}{10} - \frac{1}{5} = \frac{1}{5}$
22) $\frac{7}{8} - \frac{1}{3} = \frac{13}{24}$
23) $\frac{2}{4} - \frac{1}{4} = \frac{1}{4}$
24) $\frac{1}{2} - \frac{1}{3} = \frac{1}{6}$
25) $\frac{3}{5} - \frac{2}{5} = \frac{1}{5}$
26) $\frac{9}{10} - \frac{2}{4} = \frac{2}{5}$
27) $\frac{10}{12} - \frac{2}{3} = \frac{1}{6}$
28) $\frac{4}{8} - \frac{2}{5} = \frac{1}{10}$
29) $\frac{6}{10} - \frac{2}{4} = \frac{1}{10}$
30) $\frac{1}{2} - \frac{2}{6} = \frac{1}{6}$

Answer Key

Page 19

(1) $\frac{1}{3} - \frac{1}{8} = \frac{5}{24}$ (2) $\frac{4}{6} - \frac{1}{2} = \frac{1}{6}$ (3) $\frac{1}{2} - \frac{1}{10} = \frac{2}{5}$ (4) $\frac{2}{3} - \frac{2}{8} = \frac{5}{12}$ (5) $\frac{3}{12} - \frac{2}{9} = \frac{1}{36}$ (6) $\frac{7}{10} - \frac{2}{4} = \frac{1}{5}$

(7) $\frac{7}{8} - \frac{4}{6} = \frac{5}{24}$ (8) $\frac{1}{2} - \frac{2}{9} = \frac{5}{18}$ (9) $\frac{6}{8} - \frac{2}{5} = \frac{7}{20}$ (10) $\frac{8}{12} - \frac{2}{4} = \frac{1}{6}$ (11) $\frac{1}{6} - \frac{1}{8} = \frac{1}{24}$ (12) $\frac{4}{10} - \frac{1}{3} = \frac{1}{15}$

(13) $\frac{2}{6} - \frac{1}{4} = \frac{1}{12}$ (14) $\frac{3}{6} - \frac{1}{5} = \frac{3}{10}$ (15) $\frac{2}{3} - \frac{5}{8} = \frac{1}{24}$ (16) $\frac{5}{8} - \frac{1}{5} = \frac{17}{40}$ (17) $\frac{2}{4} - \frac{1}{3} = \frac{1}{6}$ (18) $\frac{3}{4} - \frac{3}{5} = \frac{3}{20}$

(19) $\frac{7}{8} - \frac{2}{3} = \frac{5}{24}$ (20) $\frac{3}{4} - \frac{1}{4} = \frac{1}{2}$

Page 20

(1) $\frac{3}{8} - \frac{2}{6} = \frac{1}{24}$ (2) $\frac{2}{6} - \frac{1}{4} = \frac{1}{12}$ (3) $\frac{2}{4} - \frac{1}{8} = \frac{3}{8}$ (4) $\frac{5}{6} - \frac{6}{9} = \frac{1}{6}$ (5) $\frac{5}{8} - \frac{2}{9} = \frac{29}{72}$ (6) $\frac{1}{3} - \frac{1}{5} = \frac{2}{15}$

(7) $\frac{3}{8} - \frac{1}{9} = \frac{19}{72}$ (8) $\frac{3}{4} - \frac{8}{12} = \frac{1}{12}$ (9) $\frac{2}{3} - \frac{1}{3} = \frac{1}{3}$ (10) $\frac{3}{8} - \frac{1}{5} = \frac{7}{40}$ (11) $\frac{1}{2} - \frac{1}{4} = \frac{1}{4}$ (12) $\frac{5}{6} - \frac{7}{9} = \frac{1}{18}$

(13) $\frac{2}{3} - \frac{3}{5} = \frac{1}{15}$ (14) $\frac{8}{10} - \frac{3}{5} = \frac{1}{5}$ (15) $\frac{1}{3} - \frac{1}{9} = \frac{2}{9}$ (16) $\frac{1}{2} - \frac{3}{8} = \frac{1}{8}$ (17) $\frac{8}{10} - \frac{2}{4} = \frac{3}{10}$ (18) $\frac{1}{2} - \frac{3}{9} = \frac{1}{6}$

(19) $\frac{7}{10} - \frac{2}{5} = \frac{3}{10}$ (20) $\frac{5}{8} - \frac{1}{12} = \frac{13}{24}$ (21) $\frac{3}{4} - \frac{2}{4} = \frac{1}{4}$ (22) $\frac{2}{4} - \frac{1}{9} = \frac{7}{18}$ (23) $\frac{1}{3} - \frac{1}{4} = \frac{1}{12}$ (24) $\frac{5}{6} - \frac{3}{4} = \frac{1}{12}$

(25) $\frac{5}{9} - \frac{2}{12} = \frac{7}{18}$ (26) $\frac{4}{5} - \frac{1}{5} = \frac{3}{5}$ (27) $\frac{3}{10} - \frac{1}{9} = \frac{17}{90}$ (28) $\frac{7}{9} - \frac{3}{12} = \frac{19}{36}$ (29) $\frac{3}{4} - \frac{3}{6} = \frac{1}{4}$ (30) $\frac{7}{8} - \frac{2}{8} = \frac{5}{8}$

Page 21

(1) $\frac{3}{5} \times \frac{3}{4} = \frac{9}{20}$ (2) $\frac{1}{6} \times \frac{1}{5} = \frac{1}{30}$ (3) $\frac{1}{12} \times \frac{6}{8} = \frac{1}{16}$ (4) $\frac{2}{4} \times \frac{1}{6} = \frac{1}{12}$ (5) $\frac{1}{2} \times \frac{2}{3} = \frac{1}{3}$ (6) $\frac{1}{4} \times \frac{2}{8} = \frac{1}{16}$

(7) $\frac{1}{3} \times \frac{3}{4} = \frac{1}{4}$ (8) $\frac{6}{7} \times \frac{1}{6} = \frac{1}{7}$ (9) $\frac{9}{10} \times \frac{4}{5} = \frac{18}{25}$ (10) $\frac{6}{8} \times \frac{2}{8} = \frac{3}{16}$ (11) $\frac{2}{5} \times \frac{1}{3} = \frac{2}{15}$ (12) $\frac{3}{4} \times \frac{1}{3} = \frac{1}{4}$

(13) $\frac{2}{7} \times \frac{3}{8} = \frac{3}{28}$ (14) $\frac{6}{12} \times \frac{4}{5} = \frac{2}{5}$ (15) $\frac{4}{10} \times \frac{4}{8} = \frac{1}{5}$ (16) $\frac{3}{5} \times \frac{1}{3} = \frac{1}{5}$ (17) $\frac{6}{8} \times \frac{2}{3} = \frac{1}{2}$ (18) $\frac{1}{12} \times \frac{1}{4} = \frac{1}{48}$

(19) $\frac{4}{9} \times \frac{4}{6} = \frac{8}{27}$ (20) $\frac{3}{4} \times \frac{2}{3} = \frac{1}{2}$

Page 22

(1) $\frac{3}{6} \times \frac{1}{3} = \frac{1}{6}$ (2) $\frac{3}{8} \times \frac{1}{8} = \frac{3}{64}$ (3) $\frac{1}{3} \times \frac{1}{4} = \frac{1}{12}$ (4) $\frac{3}{6} \times \frac{5}{6} = \frac{5}{12}$ (5) $\frac{3}{4} \times \frac{6}{13} = \frac{9}{26}$ (6) $\frac{5}{6} \times \frac{4}{8} = \frac{5}{12}$

(7) $\frac{1}{4} \times \frac{4}{6} = \frac{1}{6}$ (8) $\frac{4}{5} \times \frac{10}{11} = \frac{8}{11}$ (9) $\frac{1}{5} \times \frac{9}{10} = \frac{9}{50}$ (10) $\frac{3}{8} \times \frac{6}{7} = \frac{9}{28}$ (11) $\frac{1}{4} \times \frac{10}{13} = \frac{5}{26}$ (12) $\frac{4}{5} \times \frac{3}{7} = \frac{12}{35}$

(13) $\frac{5}{8} \times \frac{1}{2} = \frac{5}{16}$ (14) $\frac{2}{6} \times \frac{2}{6} = \frac{1}{9}$ (15) $\frac{2}{4} \times \frac{6}{9} = \frac{1}{3}$ (16) $\frac{1}{3} \times \frac{7}{10} = \frac{7}{30}$ (17) $\frac{2}{5} \times \frac{1}{5} = \frac{2}{25}$ (18) $\frac{1}{6} \times \frac{1}{4} = \frac{1}{24}$

(19) $\frac{2}{5} \times \frac{10}{12} = \frac{1}{3}$ (20) $\frac{1}{3} \times \frac{1}{5} = \frac{1}{15}$ (21) $\frac{1}{5} \times \frac{6}{9} = \frac{2}{15}$ (22) $\frac{2}{3} \times \frac{10}{13} = \frac{20}{39}$ (23) $\frac{4}{6} \times \frac{5}{6} = \frac{5}{9}$ (24) $\frac{4}{6} \times \frac{1}{2} = \frac{1}{3}$

(25) $\frac{4}{5} \times \frac{3}{13} = \frac{12}{65}$ (26) $\frac{1}{6} \times \frac{12}{14} = \frac{1}{7}$ (27) $\frac{1}{4} \times \frac{4}{7} = \frac{1}{7}$ (28) $\frac{1}{3} \times \frac{3}{4} = \frac{1}{4}$ (29) $\frac{2}{4} \times \frac{6}{8} = \frac{3}{8}$ (30) $\frac{4}{5} \times \frac{3}{8} = \frac{3}{10}$

Page 23

(1) $\frac{8}{9} \times \frac{2}{3} = \frac{16}{27}$ (2) $\frac{2}{8} \times \frac{1}{3} = \frac{1}{12}$ (3) $\frac{2}{7} \times \frac{4}{5} = \frac{8}{35}$ (4) $\frac{7}{11} \times \frac{3}{6} = \frac{7}{22}$ (5) $\frac{5}{10} \times \frac{1}{5} = \frac{1}{10}$ (6) $\frac{2}{9} \times \frac{2}{3} = \frac{4}{27}$

(7) $\frac{2}{4} \times \frac{2}{3} = \frac{1}{3}$ (8) $\frac{4}{6} \times \frac{3}{4} = \frac{1}{2}$ (9) $\frac{6}{10} \times \frac{1}{6} = \frac{1}{10}$ (10) $\frac{2}{5} \times \frac{1}{5} = \frac{2}{25}$ (11) $\frac{4}{11} \times \frac{2}{8} = \frac{1}{11}$ (12) $\frac{4}{7} \times \frac{1}{6} = \frac{2}{21}$

(13) $\frac{3}{9} \times \frac{3}{5} = \frac{1}{5}$ (14) $\frac{4}{6} \times \frac{2}{3} = \frac{4}{9}$ (15) $\frac{9}{10} \times \frac{2}{8} = \frac{9}{40}$ (16) $\frac{3}{4} \times \frac{1}{6} = \frac{1}{8}$ (17) $\frac{3}{7} \times \frac{4}{8} = \frac{3}{14}$ (18) $\frac{2}{3} \times \frac{4}{6} = \frac{4}{9}$

(19) $\frac{4}{5} \times \frac{1}{3} = \frac{4}{15}$ (20) $\frac{2}{10} \times \frac{2}{3} = \frac{2}{15}$

Page 24

(1) $\frac{2}{3} \times \frac{3}{5} = \frac{2}{5}$ (2) $\frac{2}{9} \times \frac{8}{12} = \frac{4}{27}$ (3) $\frac{7}{8} \times \frac{3}{12} = \frac{7}{32}$ (4) $\frac{1}{6} \times \frac{1}{5} = \frac{1}{30}$ (5) $\frac{5}{12} \times \frac{3}{8} = \frac{5}{32}$ (6) $\frac{3}{4} \times \frac{3}{9} = \frac{1}{4}$

(7) $\frac{1}{7} \times \frac{1}{2} = \frac{1}{14}$ (8) $\frac{2}{5} \times \frac{1}{10} = \frac{1}{25}$ (9) $\frac{1}{3} \times \frac{2}{9} = \frac{2}{27}$ (10) $\frac{5}{8} \times \frac{1}{2} = \frac{5}{16}$ (11) $\frac{3}{7} \times \frac{1}{11} = \frac{3}{77}$ (12) $\frac{7}{9} \times \frac{1}{4} = \frac{7}{36}$

(13) $\frac{1}{6} \times \frac{5}{10} = \frac{1}{12}$ (14) $\frac{1}{5} \times \frac{3}{5} = \frac{3}{25}$ (15) $\frac{2}{10} \times \frac{1}{2} = \frac{1}{10}$ (16) $\frac{1}{5} \times \frac{10}{11} = \frac{2}{11}$ (17) $\frac{4}{6} \times \frac{1}{3} = \frac{2}{9}$ (18) $\frac{7}{8} \times \frac{4}{8} = \frac{7}{16}$

(19) $\frac{2}{3} \times \frac{1}{7} = \frac{2}{21}$ (20) $\frac{1}{4} \times \frac{3}{10} = \frac{3}{40}$ (21) $\frac{1}{4} \times \frac{3}{4} = \frac{3}{16}$ (22) $\frac{4}{12} \times \frac{4}{5} = \frac{4}{15}$ (23) $\frac{3}{5} \times \frac{5}{12} = \frac{1}{4}$ (24) $\frac{1}{2} \times \frac{6}{7} = \frac{3}{7}$

(25) $\frac{6}{9} \times \frac{1}{3} = \frac{2}{9}$ (26) $\frac{9}{10} \times \frac{8}{11} = \frac{36}{55}$ (27) $\frac{4}{9} \times \frac{2}{9} = \frac{8}{81}$ (28) $\frac{2}{3} \times \frac{1}{2} = \frac{1}{3}$ (29) $\frac{9}{11} \times \frac{2}{3} = \frac{6}{11}$ (30) $\frac{5}{8} \times \frac{6}{12} = \frac{5}{16}$

Page 25

(1) $\frac{1}{4} \div \frac{1}{3} = \frac{3}{4}$ (2) $\frac{4}{7} \div \frac{1}{6} = \frac{24}{7}$ (3) $\frac{1}{2} \div \frac{5}{10} = \frac{1}{1}$ (4) $\frac{6}{12} \div \frac{3}{5} = \frac{5}{6}$ (5) $\frac{5}{12} \div \frac{1}{2} = \frac{5}{6}$ (6) $\frac{3}{6} \div \frac{4}{8} = \frac{1}{1}$

(7) $\frac{2}{4} \div \frac{2}{6} = \frac{3}{2}$ (8) $\frac{1}{3} \div \frac{2}{5} = \frac{5}{6}$ (9) $\frac{3}{9} \div \frac{4}{10} = \frac{5}{6}$ (10) $\frac{1}{6} \div \frac{4}{5} = \frac{5}{24}$ (11) $\frac{7}{10} \div \frac{1}{2} = \frac{7}{5}$ (12) $\frac{2}{4} \div \frac{2}{3} = \frac{3}{4}$

(13) $\frac{4}{5} \div \frac{5}{10} = \frac{8}{5}$ (14) $\frac{5}{9} \div \frac{3}{6} = \frac{10}{9}$ (15) $\frac{3}{12} \div \frac{2}{5} = \frac{5}{8}$ (16) $\frac{3}{6} \div \frac{1}{2} = \frac{1}{1}$ (17) $\frac{1}{2} \div \frac{2}{4} = \frac{1}{1}$ (18) $\frac{5}{7} \div \frac{2}{3} = \frac{15}{14}$

(19) $\frac{5}{10} \div \frac{4}{10} = \frac{5}{4}$ (20) $\frac{10}{12} \div \frac{1}{5} = \frac{25}{6}$

Page 26

(1) $\frac{2}{3} \div \frac{3}{5} = \frac{10}{9}$ (2) $\frac{3}{9} \div \frac{1}{2} = \frac{2}{3}$ (3) $\frac{6}{7} \div \frac{3}{7} = \frac{2}{1}$ (4) $\frac{1}{2} \div \frac{1}{3} = \frac{3}{2}$ (5) $\frac{1}{3} \div \frac{3}{9} = \frac{1}{1}$ (6) $\frac{3}{6} \div \frac{1}{5} = \frac{5}{2}$

(7) $\frac{1}{5} \div \frac{3}{6} = \frac{2}{5}$ (8) $\frac{6}{9} \div \frac{4}{5} = \frac{5}{6}$ (9) $\frac{3}{7} \div \frac{3}{7} = \frac{1}{1}$ (10) $\frac{3}{4} \div \frac{1}{2} = \frac{3}{2}$ (11) $\frac{4}{8} \div \frac{4}{7} = \frac{7}{8}$ (12) $\frac{3}{4} \div \frac{1}{3} = \frac{9}{4}$

(13) $\frac{4}{7} \div \frac{2}{8} = \frac{16}{7}$ (14) $\frac{7}{9} \div \frac{2}{9} = \frac{7}{2}$ (15) $\frac{1}{6} \div \frac{3}{4} = \frac{2}{9}$ (16) $\frac{1}{3} \div \frac{3}{7} = \frac{7}{9}$ (17) $\frac{6}{8} \div \frac{7}{8} = \frac{6}{7}$ (18) $\frac{1}{4} \div \frac{6}{9} = \frac{3}{8}$

(19) $\frac{6}{8} \div \frac{1}{2} = \frac{3}{2}$ (20) $\frac{1}{6} \div \frac{1}{5} = \frac{5}{6}$ (21) $\frac{1}{5} \div \frac{1}{8} = \frac{8}{5}$ (22) $\frac{1}{3} \div \frac{1}{7} = \frac{7}{3}$ (23) $\frac{1}{7} \div \frac{1}{2} = \frac{2}{7}$ (24) $\frac{3}{8} \div \frac{1}{8} = \frac{3}{1}$

(25) $\frac{2}{4} \div \frac{1}{6} = \frac{3}{1}$ (26) $\frac{1}{2} \div \frac{6}{8} = \frac{2}{3}$ (27) $\frac{4}{7} \div \frac{7}{9} = \frac{36}{49}$ (28) $\frac{1}{2} \div \frac{1}{4} = \frac{2}{1}$ (29) $\frac{7}{9} \div \frac{1}{2} = \frac{14}{9}$ (30) $\frac{7}{8} \div \frac{4}{5} = \frac{35}{32}$

Page 27

(1) $\frac{1}{5} \div \frac{1}{4} = \frac{4}{5}$ (2) $\frac{1}{2} \div \frac{1}{2} = \frac{1}{1}$ (3) $\frac{1}{4} \div \frac{6}{8} = \frac{1}{3}$ (4) $\frac{6}{8} \div \frac{4}{6} = \frac{9}{8}$ (5) $\frac{5}{9} \div \frac{2}{5} = \frac{25}{18}$ (6) $\frac{1}{2} \div \frac{2}{7} = \frac{7}{4}$

(7) $\frac{2}{6} \div \frac{1}{4} = \frac{4}{3}$ (8) $\frac{3}{5} \div \frac{2}{5} = \frac{3}{2}$ (9) $\frac{1}{2} \div \frac{3}{8} = \frac{4}{3}$ (10) $\frac{2}{3} \div \frac{1}{2} = \frac{4}{3}$ (11) $\frac{5}{10} \div \frac{7}{8} = \frac{4}{7}$ (12) $\frac{1}{4} \div \frac{2}{4} = \frac{1}{2}$

(13) $\frac{2}{5} \div \frac{1}{2} = \frac{4}{5}$ (14) $\frac{2}{3} \div \frac{4}{8} = \frac{4}{3}$ (15) $\frac{7}{9} \div \frac{3}{5} = \frac{35}{27}$ (16) $\frac{1}{2} \div \frac{1}{3} = \frac{3}{2}$ (17) $\frac{1}{2} \div \frac{2}{4} = \frac{1}{1}$ (18) $\frac{7}{10} \div \frac{1}{6} = \frac{21}{5}$

(19) $\frac{2}{8} \div \frac{2}{3} = \frac{3}{8}$ (20) $\frac{5}{6} \div \frac{2}{3} = \frac{5}{4}$

Page 28

(1) $\frac{3}{4} \div \frac{1}{2} = \frac{3}{2}$ (2) $\frac{2}{3} \div \frac{2}{3} = \frac{1}{1}$ (3) $\frac{3}{6} \div \frac{6}{8} = \frac{2}{3}$ (4) $\frac{4}{5} \div \frac{1}{5} = \frac{4}{1}$ (5) $\frac{2}{4} \div \frac{1}{4} = \frac{2}{1}$ (6) $\frac{2}{3} \div \frac{1}{6} = \frac{4}{1}$

(7) $\frac{1}{3} \div \frac{4}{8} = \frac{2}{3}$ (8) $\frac{1}{2} \div \frac{1}{2} = \frac{1}{1}$ (9) $\frac{2}{5} \div \frac{4}{6} = \frac{3}{5}$ (10) $\frac{3}{4} \div \frac{1}{4} = \frac{3}{1}$ (11) $\frac{1}{5} \div \frac{4}{8} = \frac{2}{5}$ (12) $\frac{1}{3} \div \frac{7}{8} = \frac{8}{21}$

(13) $\frac{4}{5} \div \frac{1}{4} = \frac{16}{5}$ (14) $\frac{3}{4} \div \frac{3}{5} = \frac{5}{4}$ (15) $\frac{4}{6} \div \frac{2}{8} = \frac{8}{3}$ (16) $\frac{1}{2} \div \frac{3}{6} = \frac{1}{1}$ (17) $\frac{3}{5} \div \frac{3}{6} = \frac{6}{5}$ (18) $\frac{1}{2} \div \frac{7}{8} = \frac{4}{7}$

(19) $\frac{2}{5} \div \frac{2}{3} = \frac{3}{5}$ (20) $\frac{5}{8} \div \frac{7}{8} = \frac{5}{7}$ (21) $\frac{4}{6} \div \frac{1}{2} = \frac{4}{3}$ (22) $\frac{1}{2} \div \frac{1}{3} = \frac{3}{2}$ (23) $\frac{2}{8} \div \frac{1}{2} = \frac{1}{2}$ (24) $\frac{1}{3} \div \frac{1}{4} = \frac{4}{3}$

(25) $\frac{5}{6} \div \frac{2}{8} = \frac{10}{3}$ (26) $\frac{1}{2} \div \frac{2}{5} = \frac{5}{4}$ (27) $\frac{2}{5} \div \frac{2}{8} = \frac{8}{5}$ (28) $\frac{1}{2} \div \frac{4}{6} = \frac{3}{4}$ (29) $\frac{1}{6} \div \frac{1}{3} = \frac{1}{2}$ (30) $\frac{3}{6} \div \frac{1}{2} = \frac{1}{1}$

Page 29

(1) $6\frac{3}{4} = \frac{27}{4}$ (2) $4\frac{1}{2} = \frac{9}{2}$ (3) $7\frac{2}{4} = \frac{15}{2}$ (4) $6\frac{2}{5} = \frac{32}{5}$ (5) $7\frac{1}{3} = \frac{22}{3}$ (6) $1\frac{1}{2} = \frac{3}{2}$

(7) $8\frac{2}{4} = \frac{17}{2}$ (8) $8\frac{1}{2} = \frac{17}{2}$ (9) $2\frac{3}{6} = \frac{5}{2}$ (10) $7\frac{1}{5} = \frac{36}{5}$ (11) $9\frac{1}{3} = \frac{28}{3}$ (12) $7\frac{4}{8} = \frac{15}{2}$

(13) $1\frac{5}{6} = \frac{11}{6}$ (14) $3\frac{2}{3} = \frac{11}{3}$ (15) $4\frac{4}{6} = \frac{14}{3}$ (16) $7\frac{1}{2} = \frac{15}{2}$ (17) $7\frac{2}{3} = \frac{23}{3}$ (18) $9\frac{2}{4} = \frac{19}{2}$

(19) $8\frac{1}{4} = \frac{33}{4}$ (20) $9\frac{5}{6} = \frac{59}{6}$

Page 30

(1) $4\frac{5}{16} = \frac{69}{16}$ (2) $2\frac{3}{6} = \frac{5}{2}$ (3) $4\frac{7}{8} = \frac{39}{8}$ (4) $3\frac{5}{6} = \frac{23}{6}$ (5) $3\frac{3}{4} = \frac{15}{4}$ (6) $2\frac{4}{6} = \frac{8}{3}$

(7) $2\frac{2}{6} = \frac{7}{3}$ (8) $1\frac{4}{6} = \frac{5}{3}$ (9) $6\frac{13}{18} = \frac{121}{18}$ (10) $7\frac{2}{4} = \frac{15}{2}$ (11) $5\frac{1}{9} = \frac{46}{9}$ (12) $8\frac{5}{8} = \frac{69}{8}$

(13) $2\frac{5}{6} = \frac{17}{6}$ (14) $7\frac{1}{2} = \frac{15}{2}$ (15) $6\frac{8}{12} = \frac{20}{3}$ (16) $3\frac{2}{4} = \frac{7}{2}$ (17) $5\frac{2}{18} = \frac{46}{9}$ (18) $3\frac{1}{3} = \frac{10}{3}$

(19) $2\frac{9}{12} = \frac{11}{4}$ (20) $2\frac{1}{2} = \frac{5}{2}$ (21) $6\frac{1}{4} = \frac{25}{4}$ (22) $1\frac{2}{5} = \frac{7}{5}$ (23) $3\frac{2}{16} = \frac{25}{8}$ (24) $5\frac{2}{4} = \frac{11}{2}$

(25) $7\frac{17}{18} = \frac{143}{18}$ (26) $7\frac{4}{12} = \frac{22}{3}$ (27) $5\frac{4}{8} = \frac{11}{2}$ (28) $4\frac{6}{10} = \frac{23}{5}$ (29) $2\frac{2}{4} = \frac{5}{2}$ (30) $4\frac{2}{4} = \frac{9}{2}$

Page 31

1) $9\frac{5}{6} = \frac{59}{6}$ 2) $6\frac{1}{3} = \frac{19}{3}$ 3) $6\frac{3}{5} = \frac{33}{5}$ 4) $5\frac{4}{8} = \frac{11}{2}$ 5) $2\frac{1}{6} = \frac{13}{6}$ 6) $4\frac{1}{4} = \frac{17}{4}$ 7) $3\frac{1}{3} = \frac{10}{3}$

8) $8\frac{4}{6} = \frac{26}{3}$ 9) $9\frac{2}{3} = \frac{29}{3}$ 10) $5\frac{2}{4} = \frac{11}{2}$ 11) $4\frac{3}{5} = \frac{23}{5}$ 12) $4\frac{2}{6} = \frac{13}{3}$ 13) $1\frac{3}{5} = \frac{8}{5}$ 14) $7\frac{7}{8} = \frac{63}{8}$

15) $3\frac{3}{4} = \frac{15}{4}$ 16) $9\frac{1}{4} = \frac{37}{4}$ 17) $7\frac{1}{5} = \frac{36}{5}$ 18) $3\frac{5}{6} = \frac{23}{6}$ 19) $6\frac{2}{3} = \frac{20}{3}$ 20) $6\frac{4}{5} = \frac{34}{5}$

Page 32

1) $9\frac{2}{4} = \frac{19}{2}$ 2) $7\frac{2}{3} = \frac{23}{3}$ 3) $2\frac{4}{6} = \frac{8}{3}$ 4) $2\frac{5}{6} = \frac{17}{6}$ 5) $6\frac{1}{4} = \frac{25}{4}$ 6) $2\frac{2}{3} = \frac{8}{3}$ 7) $1\frac{7}{9} = \frac{16}{9}$

8) $8\frac{1}{5} = \frac{41}{5}$ 9) $3\frac{7}{8} = \frac{31}{8}$ 10) $8\frac{2}{3} = \frac{26}{3}$ 11) $3\frac{4}{9} = \frac{31}{9}$ 12) $7\frac{1}{2} = \frac{15}{2}$ 13) $5\frac{5}{8} = \frac{45}{8}$ 14) $3\frac{3}{6} = \frac{7}{2}$

15) $8\frac{1}{2} = \frac{17}{2}$ 16) $7\frac{4}{5} = \frac{39}{5}$ 17) $5\frac{2}{4} = \frac{11}{2}$ 18) $8\frac{1}{3} = \frac{25}{3}$ 19) $5\frac{2}{3} = \frac{17}{3}$ 20) $1\frac{6}{8} = \frac{7}{4}$ 21) $6\frac{4}{5} = \frac{34}{5}$

22) $1\frac{1}{2} = \frac{3}{2}$ 23) $5\frac{7}{8} = \frac{47}{8}$ 24) $3\frac{5}{9} = \frac{32}{9}$ 25) $5\frac{3}{5} = \frac{28}{5}$ 26) $4\frac{1}{2} = \frac{9}{2}$ 27) $9\frac{5}{8} = \frac{77}{8}$ 28) $6\frac{2}{4} = \frac{13}{2}$

29) $4\frac{3}{9} = \frac{13}{3}$ 30) $9\frac{2}{3} = \frac{29}{3}$

Page 33

1) $\frac{4}{3} = 1\frac{1}{3}$ 2) $\frac{22}{6} = 3\frac{2}{3}$ 3) $\frac{10}{4} = 2\frac{1}{2}$ 4) $\frac{25}{3} = 8\frac{1}{3}$ 5) $\frac{19}{3} = 6\frac{1}{3}$ 6) $\frac{46}{6} = 7\frac{2}{3}$ 7) $\frac{33}{4} = 8\frac{1}{4}$

8) $\frac{31}{6} = 5\frac{1}{6}$ 9) $\frac{50}{6} = 8\frac{1}{3}$ 10) $\frac{11}{4} = 2\frac{3}{4}$ 11) $\frac{33}{8} = 4\frac{1}{8}$ 12) $\frac{6}{5} = 1\frac{1}{5}$ 13) $\frac{20}{6} = 3\frac{1}{3}$ 14) $\frac{7}{3} = 2\frac{1}{3}$

15) $\frac{29}{3} = 9\frac{2}{3}$ 16) $\frac{37}{5} = 7\frac{2}{5}$ 17) $\frac{19}{6} = 3\frac{1}{6}$ 18) $\frac{11}{5} = 2\frac{1}{5}$ 19) $\frac{62}{8} = 7\frac{3}{4}$ 20) $\frac{29}{8} = 3\frac{5}{8}$

Page 34

1) $\frac{48}{5} = 9\frac{3}{5}$ 2) $\frac{25}{6} = 4\frac{1}{6}$ 3) $\frac{9}{8} = 1\frac{1}{8}$ 4) $\frac{22}{3} = 7\frac{1}{3}$ 5) $\frac{52}{6} = 8\frac{2}{3}$ 6) $\frac{22}{4} = 5\frac{1}{2}$ 7) $\frac{26}{3} = 8\frac{2}{3}$

8) $\frac{29}{5} = 5\frac{4}{5}$ 9) $\frac{10}{4} = 2\frac{1}{2}$ 10) $\frac{28}{8} = 3\frac{1}{2}$ 11) $\frac{25}{8} = 3\frac{1}{8}$ 12) $\frac{16}{6} = 2\frac{2}{3}$ 13) $\frac{43}{5} = 8\frac{3}{5}$ 14) $\frac{29}{8} = 3\frac{5}{8}$

15) $\frac{11}{4} = 2\frac{3}{4}$ 16) $\frac{10}{8} = 1\frac{1}{4}$ 17) $\frac{11}{3} = 3\frac{2}{3}$ 18) $\frac{49}{6} = 8\frac{1}{6}$ 19) $\frac{16}{3} = 5\frac{1}{3}$ 20) $\frac{23}{4} = 5\frac{3}{4}$ 21) $\frac{31}{4} = 7\frac{3}{4}$

22) $\frac{36}{8} = 4\frac{1}{2}$ 23) $\frac{13}{3} = 4\frac{1}{3}$ 24) $\frac{37}{5} = 7\frac{2}{5}$ 25) $\frac{7}{4} = 1\frac{3}{4}$ 26) $\frac{20}{3} = 6\frac{2}{3}$ 27) $\frac{29}{6} = 4\frac{5}{6}$ 28) $\frac{46}{5} = 9\frac{1}{5}$

29) $\frac{32}{6} = 5\frac{1}{3}$ 30) $\frac{39}{8} = 4\frac{7}{8}$

Page 35

1) $\frac{9}{5} = 1\frac{4}{5}$ 2) $\frac{19}{2} = 9\frac{1}{2}$ 3) $\frac{86}{9} = 9\frac{5}{9}$ 4) $\frac{14}{8} = 1\frac{3}{4}$ 5) $\frac{37}{4} = 9\frac{1}{4}$ 6) $\frac{35}{9} = 3\frac{8}{9}$ 7) $\frac{11}{5} = 2\frac{1}{5}$

8) $\frac{35}{6} = 5\frac{5}{6}$ 9) $\frac{9}{2} = 4\frac{1}{2}$ 10) $\frac{17}{3} = 5\frac{2}{3}$ 11) $\frac{48}{5} = 9\frac{3}{5}$ 12) $\frac{62}{8} = 7\frac{3}{4}$ 13) $\frac{17}{2} = 8\frac{1}{2}$ 14) $\frac{27}{4} = 6\frac{3}{4}$

15) $\frac{17}{8} = 2\frac{1}{8}$ 16) $\frac{26}{3} = 8\frac{2}{3}$ 17) $\frac{47}{5} = 9\frac{2}{5}$ 18) $\frac{48}{9} = 5\frac{1}{3}$ 19) $\frac{15}{4} = 3\frac{3}{4}$ 20) $\frac{13}{3} = 4\frac{1}{3}$

Page 36

1) $\frac{48}{5} = 9\frac{3}{5}$ 2) $\frac{11}{3} = 3\frac{2}{3}$ 3) $\frac{31}{8} = 3\frac{7}{8}$ 4) $\frac{74}{9} = 8\frac{2}{9}$ 5) $\frac{16}{5} = 3\frac{1}{5}$ 6) $\frac{8}{5} = 1\frac{3}{5}$ 7) $\frac{25}{3} = 8\frac{1}{3}$

8) $\frac{63}{8} = 7\frac{7}{8}$ 9) $\frac{11}{2} = 5\frac{1}{2}$ 10) $\frac{34}{6} = 5\frac{2}{3}$ 11) $\frac{25}{4} = 6\frac{1}{4}$ 12) $\frac{23}{3} = 7\frac{2}{3}$ 13) $\frac{46}{5} = 9\frac{1}{5}$ 14) $\frac{15}{6} = 2\frac{1}{2}$

15) $\frac{11}{5} = 2\frac{1}{5}$ 16) $\frac{30}{4} = 7\frac{1}{2}$ 17) $\frac{27}{5} = 5\frac{2}{5}$ 18) $\frac{58}{8} = 7\frac{1}{4}$ 19) $\frac{71}{9} = 7\frac{8}{9}$ 20) $\frac{10}{3} = 3\frac{1}{3}$ 21) $\frac{5}{2} = 2\frac{1}{2}$

22) $\frac{22}{3} = 7\frac{1}{3}$ 23) $\frac{45}{6} = 7\frac{1}{2}$ 24) $\frac{11}{4} = 2\frac{3}{4}$ 25) $\frac{8}{3} = 2\frac{2}{3}$ 26) $\frac{42}{9} = 4\frac{2}{3}$ 27) $\frac{33}{8} = 4\frac{1}{8}$ 28) $\frac{82}{9} = 9\frac{1}{9}$

29) $\frac{17}{2} = 8\frac{1}{2}$ 30) $\frac{14}{8} = 1\frac{3}{4}$

Answer Key

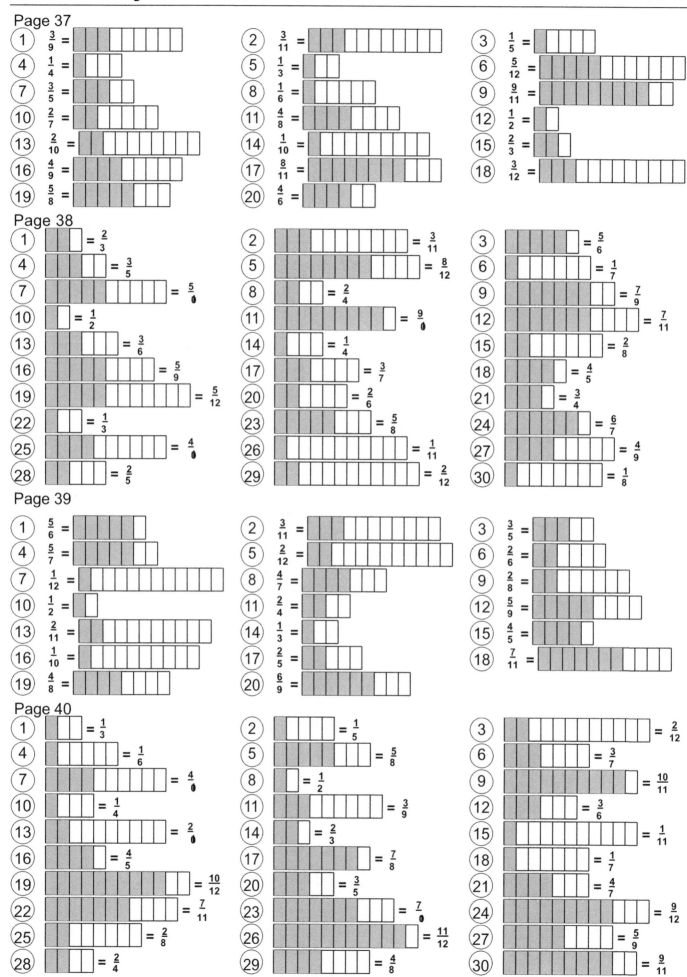

Page 37

1) $\frac{3}{9}$ =

2) $\frac{3}{11}$ =

3) $\frac{1}{5}$ =

4) $\frac{1}{4}$ =

5) $\frac{1}{3}$ =

6) $\frac{5}{12}$ =

7) $\frac{3}{5}$ =

8) $\frac{1}{6}$ =

9) $\frac{9}{11}$ =

10) $\frac{2}{7}$ =

11) $\frac{4}{8}$ =

12) $\frac{1}{2}$ =

13) $\frac{2}{10}$ =

14) $\frac{1}{10}$ =

15) $\frac{2}{3}$ =

16) $\frac{4}{9}$ =

17) $\frac{8}{11}$ =

18) $\frac{3}{12}$ =

19) $\frac{5}{8}$ =

20) $\frac{4}{6}$ =

Page 38

1) = $\frac{2}{3}$

2) = $\frac{3}{11}$

3) = $\frac{5}{6}$

4) = $\frac{3}{5}$

5) = $\frac{8}{12}$

6) = $\frac{1}{7}$

7) = $\frac{5}{6}$

8) = $\frac{2}{4}$

9) = $\frac{7}{9}$

10) = $\frac{1}{2}$

11) = $\frac{9}{6}$

12) = $\frac{7}{11}$

13) = $\frac{3}{6}$

14) = $\frac{1}{4}$

15) = $\frac{2}{8}$

16) = $\frac{5}{9}$

17) = $\frac{3}{7}$

18) = $\frac{4}{5}$

19) = $\frac{5}{12}$

20) = $\frac{2}{6}$

21) = $\frac{3}{4}$

22) = $\frac{1}{3}$

23) = $\frac{5}{8}$

24) = $\frac{6}{7}$

25) = $\frac{4}{6}$

26) = $\frac{1}{11}$

27) = $\frac{4}{9}$

28) = $\frac{2}{5}$

29) = $\frac{2}{12}$

30) = $\frac{1}{8}$

Page 39

1) $\frac{5}{6}$ =

2) $\frac{3}{11}$ =

3) $\frac{3}{5}$ =

4) $\frac{5}{7}$ =

5) $\frac{2}{12}$ =

6) $\frac{2}{6}$ =

7) $\frac{1}{12}$ =

8) $\frac{4}{7}$ =

9) $\frac{2}{8}$ =

10) $\frac{1}{2}$ =

11) $\frac{2}{4}$ =

12) $\frac{5}{9}$ =

13) $\frac{2}{11}$ =

14) $\frac{1}{3}$ =

15) $\frac{4}{5}$ =

16) $\frac{1}{10}$ =

17) $\frac{2}{5}$ =

18) $\frac{7}{11}$ =

19) $\frac{4}{8}$ =

20) $\frac{6}{9}$ =

Page 40

1) = $\frac{1}{3}$

2) = $\frac{1}{5}$

3) = $\frac{2}{12}$

4) = $\frac{1}{6}$

5) = $\frac{5}{8}$

6) = $\frac{3}{7}$

7) = $\frac{4}{6}$

8) = $\frac{1}{2}$

9) = $\frac{10}{11}$

10) = $\frac{1}{4}$

11) = $\frac{3}{9}$

12) = $\frac{3}{6}$

13) = $\frac{2}{6}$

14) = $\frac{2}{3}$

15) = $\frac{1}{11}$

16) = $\frac{4}{5}$

17) = $\frac{7}{8}$

18) = $\frac{1}{7}$

19) = $\frac{10}{12}$

20) = $\frac{3}{5}$

21) = $\frac{4}{7}$

22) = $\frac{7}{11}$

23) = $\frac{7}{6}$

24) = $\frac{9}{12}$

25) = $\frac{2}{8}$

26) = $\frac{11}{12}$

27) = $\frac{5}{9}$

28) = $\frac{2}{4}$

29) = $\frac{4}{8}$

30) = $\frac{9}{11}$

Answer Key

Page 41

1. $\frac{1}{2} = 0.5$
2. $\frac{3}{5} = 0.6$
3. $\frac{1}{3} = 0.333$
4. $\frac{4}{6} = 0.667$
5. $\frac{5}{9} = 0.556$
6. $\frac{2}{3} = 0.667$
7. $\frac{3}{4} = 0.75$
8. $\frac{7}{9} = 0.778$
9. $\frac{5}{10} = 0.5$
10. $\frac{1}{5} = 0.2$
11. $\frac{1}{8} = 0.125$
12. $\frac{2}{8} = 0.25$
13. $\frac{2}{6} = 0.333$
14. $\frac{3}{10} = 0.3$
15. $\frac{2}{5} = 0.4$
16. $\frac{1}{4} = 0.25$
17. $\frac{6}{9} = 0.667$
18. $\frac{2}{10} = 0.2$
19. $\frac{3}{9} = 0.333$
20. $\frac{4}{8} = 0.5$

Page 42

1. $\frac{3}{8} = 0.375$
2. $\frac{3}{5} = 0.6$
3. $\frac{1}{2} = 0.5$
4. $\frac{3}{4} = 0.75$
5. $\frac{2}{9} = 0.222$
6. $\frac{2}{6} = 0.333$
7. $\frac{2}{3} = 0.667$
8. $\frac{3}{10} = 0.3$
9. $\frac{1}{8} = 0.125$
10. $\frac{4}{8} = 0.5$
11. $\frac{7}{10} = 0.7$
12. $\frac{2}{4} = 0.5$
13. $\frac{5}{6} = 0.833$
14. $\frac{1}{10} = 0.1$
15. $\frac{7}{9} = 0.778$
16. $\frac{1}{5} = 0.2$
17. $\frac{4}{5} = 0.8$
18. $\frac{8}{9} = 0.889$
19. $\frac{1}{3} = 0.333$
20. $\frac{9}{10} = 0.9$
21. $\frac{5}{8} = 0.625$
22. $\frac{5}{10} = 0.5$
23. $\frac{4}{6} = 0.667$
24. $\frac{2}{5} = 0.4$
25. $\frac{8}{10} = 0.8$
26. $\frac{7}{8} = 0.875$
27. $\frac{1}{4} = 0.25$
28. $\frac{2}{8} = 0.25$
29. $\frac{5}{9} = 0.556$
30. $\frac{4}{9} = 0.444$

Page 43

1. $\frac{1}{10} = 0.1$
2. $\frac{5}{6} = 0.833$
3. $\frac{3}{9} = 0.333$
4. $\frac{2}{5} = 0.4$
5. $\frac{3}{4} = 0.75$
6. $\frac{9}{10} = 0.9$
7. $\frac{2}{3} = 0.667$
8. $\frac{1}{2} = 0.5$
9. $\frac{4}{8} = 0.5$
10. $\frac{3}{10} = 0.3$
11. $\frac{2}{4} = 0.5$
12. $\frac{8}{9} = 0.889$
13. $\frac{4}{6} = 0.667$
14. $\frac{1}{3} = 0.333$
15. $\frac{1}{5} = 0.2$
16. $\frac{1}{8} = 0.125$
17. $\frac{5}{9} = 0.556$
18. $\frac{5}{8} = 0.625$
19. $\frac{3}{6} = 0.5$
20. $\frac{4}{5} = 0.8$

Page 44

1. $\frac{1}{4} = 0.25$
2. $\frac{4}{9} = 0.444$
3. $\frac{1}{6} = 0.167$
4. $\frac{3}{5} = 0.6$
5. $\frac{3}{10} = 0.3$
6. $\frac{1}{2} = 0.5$
7. $\frac{1}{3} = 0.333$
8. $\frac{4}{6} = 0.667$
9. $\frac{7}{8} = 0.875$
10. $\frac{5}{10} = 0.5$
11. $\frac{2}{4} = 0.5$
12. $\frac{6}{9} = 0.667$
13. $\frac{3}{6} = 0.5$
14. $\frac{2}{9} = 0.222$
15. $\frac{6}{10} = 0.6$
16. $\frac{3}{9} = 0.333$
17. $\frac{4}{8} = 0.5$
18. $\frac{4}{10} = 0.4$
19. $\frac{5}{8} = 0.625$
20. $\frac{2}{3} = 0.667$
21. $\frac{2}{10} = 0.2$
22. $\frac{3}{4} = 0.75$
23. $\frac{2}{5} = 0.4$
24. $\frac{5}{9} = 0.556$
25. $\frac{1}{10} = 0.1$
26. $\frac{4}{5} = 0.8$
27. $\frac{2}{8} = 0.25$
28. $\frac{6}{8} = 0.75$
29. $\frac{1}{5} = 0.2$
30. $\frac{7}{10} = 0.7$

Page 45

1. $0.085 + 0.014 = 0.099$
2. $0.05 + 1.62 = 1.67$
3. $0.41 + 0.01 = 0.42$
4. $0.2 + 3.2 = 3.4$
5. $0.03 + 1.49 = 1.52$
6. $0.005 + 0.023 = 0.028$
7. $8.6 + 16.2 = 24.8$
8. $0.4 + 18.2 = 18.6$
9. $0.05 + 1.68 = 1.73$
10. $0.054 + 0.056 = 0.110$
11. $0.007 + 0.061 = 0.068$
12. $4.9 + 5.8 = 10.7$
13. $8.6 + 15.1 = 23.7$
14. $3.6 + 3.3 = 6.9$
15. $0.039 + 0.124 = 0.163$
16. $0.9 + 16.1 = 17.0$
17. $3.7 + 10.1 = 13.8$
18. $0.05 + 1.38 = 1.43$
19. $0.031 + 0.082 = 0.113$
20. $0.09 + 1.96 = 2.05$

Page 46

1. $14.4 + 6.8 = 21.2$
2. $1.64 + 0.14 = 1.78$
3. $12.2 + 5.9 = 18.1$
4. $16.6 + 0.4 = 17.0$
5. $8.3 + 7.4 = 15.7$
6. $14.5 + 9.0 = 23.5$
7. $16.4 + 5.8 = 22.2$
8. $15.6 + 6.6 = 22.2$
9. $15.4 + 4.6 = 20.0$
10. $0.119 + 0.049 = 0.168$
11. $1.59 + 0.93 = 2.52$
12. $19.5 + 4.9 = 24.4$
13. $10.7 + 4.9 = 15.6$
14. $0.079 + 0.044 = 0.123$
15. $0.048 + 0.011 = 0.059$
16. $0.124 + 0.003 = 0.127$

(17)
```
  0.82
+ 0.95
------
  1.77
```
(18)
```
  13.6
+  4.0
------
  17.6
```
(19)
```
  0.118
+ 0.021
------
  0.139
```
(20)
```
  7.6
+ 4.7
-----
 12.3
```
(21)
```
  10.4
+  0.9
-----
  11.3
```
(22)
```
  0.067
+ 0.034
------
  0.101
```
(23)
```
  1.90
+ 0.47
-----
  2.37
```
(24)
```
  0.068
+ 0.022
------
  0.090
```

(25)
```
  8.6
+ 9.7
-----
 18.3
```
(26)
```
  0.82
+ 0.85
------
  1.67
```
(27)
```
  0.94
+ 0.98
------
  1.92
```
(28)
```
  0.82
+ 0.79
------
  1.61
```
(29)
```
  1.40
+ 0.34
------
  1.74
```
(30)
```
  12.1
+  1.3
-----
  13.4
```

Page 47

(1)
```
  1.5
+ 1.3
-----
  2.8
```
(2)
```
  0.5
+ 0.8
-----
  1.3
```
(3)
```
  0.11
+ 0.07
------
  0.18
```
(4)
```
  0.06
+ 0.13
------
  0.19
```
(5)
```
  0.08
+ 0.09
------
  0.17
```
(6)
```
  0.003
+ 0.006
------
  0.009
```
(7)
```
  0.012
+ 0.003
------
  0.015
```
(8)
```
  0.6
+ 0.8
-----
  1.4
```

(9)
```
  0.002
+ 0.013
------
  0.015
```
(10)
```
  0.6
+ 2.0
-----
  2.6
```
(11)
```
  0.6
+ 1.4
-----
  2.0
```
(12)
```
  0.06
+ 0.03
------
  0.09
```
(13)
```
  0.11
+ 0.20
------
  0.31
```
(14)
```
  1.7
+ 1.4
-----
  3.1
```
(15)
```
  0.006
+ 0.004
------
  0.010
```
(16)
```
  0.019
+ 0.009
------
  0.028
```

(17)
```
  1.2
+ 1.8
-----
  3.0
```
(18)
```
  0.8
+ 1.2
-----
  2.0
```
(19)
```
  0.018
+ 0.018
------
  0.036
```
(20)
```
  0.1
+ 0.7
-----
  0.8
```

Page 48

(1)
```
  0.11
+ 0.10
------
  0.21
```
(2)
```
  0.005
+ 0.020
------
  0.025
```
(3)
```
  0.009
+ 0.019
------
  0.028
```
(4)
```
  0.10
+ 0.05
------
  0.15
```
(5)
```
  0.03
+ 0.04
------
  0.07
```
(6)
```
  0.019
+ 0.019
------
  0.038
```
(7)
```
  1.6
+ 1.1
-----
  2.7
```
(8)
```
  1.3
+ 0.6
-----
  1.9
```

(9)
```
  0.12
+ 0.01
------
  0.13
```
(10)
```
  0.08
+ 0.02
------
  0.10
```
(11)
```
  0.5
+ 1.0
-----
  1.5
```
(12)
```
  0.9
+ 1.2
-----
  2.1
```
(13)
```
  0.001
+ 0.004
------
  0.005
```
(14)
```
  0.011
+ 0.008
------
  0.019
```
(15)
```
  0.002
+ 0.017
------
  0.019
```
(16)
```
  0.6
+ 0.4
-----
  1.0
```

(17)
```
  1.7
+ 0.8
-----
  2.5
```
(18)
```
  1.7
+ 1.0
-----
  2.7
```
(19)
```
  0.001
+ 0.017
------
  0.018
```
(20)
```
  0.6
+ 0.7
-----
  1.3
```
(21)
```
  0.011
+ 0.004
------
  0.015
```
(22)
```
  0.019
+ 0.011
------
  0.030
```
(23)
```
  0.019
+ 0.005
------
  0.024
```
(24)
```
  1.8
+ 1.7
-----
  3.5
```

(25)
```
  0.006
+ 0.003
------
  0.009
```
(26)
```
  0.006
+ 0.011
------
  0.017
```
(27)
```
  0.012
+ 0.004
------
  0.016
```
(28)
```
  1.1
+ 1.6
-----
  2.7
```
(29)
```
  0.008
+ 0.019
------
  0.027
```
(30)
```
  0.018
+ 0.009
------
  0.027
```

Page 49

(1)
```
  0.67
- 0.29
------
  0.38
```
(2)
```
  0.051
- 0.021
------
  0.030
```
(3)
```
  0.56
- 0.41
------
  0.15
```
(4)
```
  8.5
- 7.6
-----
  0.9
```
(5)
```
  8.0
- 3.2
-----
  4.8
```
(6)
```
  0.086
- 0.060
------
  0.026
```
(7)
```
  0.80
- 0.72
------
  0.08
```
(8)
```
  0.45
- 0.21
------
  0.24
```

(9)
```
  7.2
- 5.8
-----
  1.4
```
(10)
```
  8.1
- 3.7
-----
  4.4
```
(11)
```
  0.082
- 0.075
------
  0.007
```
(12)
```
  0.51
- 0.04
------
  0.47
```
(13)
```
  0.043
- 0.016
------
  0.027
```
(14)
```
  0.75
- 0.66
------
  0.09
```
(15)
```
  0.077
- 0.025
------
  0.052
```
(16)
```
  5.2
- 4.9
-----
  0.3
```

(17)
```
  2.0
- 0.1
-----
  1.9
```
(18)
```
  3.9
- 1.5
-----
  2.4
```
(19)
```
  0.75
- 0.29
------
  0.46
```
(20)
```
  0.61
- 0.50
------
  0.11
```

Page 50

(1)
```
  0.17
- 0.05
------
  0.12
```
(2)
```
  0.15
- 0.12
------
  0.03
```
(3)
```
  0.015
- 0.009
------
  0.006
```
(4)
```
  0.006
- 0.001
------
  0.005
```
(5)
```
  0.016
- 0.014
------
  0.002
```
(6)
```
  0.04
- 0.02
------
  0.02
```
(7)
```
  0.17
- 0.10
------
  0.07
```
(8)
```
  1.3
- 0.3
-----
  1.0
```

(9)
```
  0.14
- 0.04
------
  0.10
```
(10)
```
  0.20
- 0.12
------
  0.08
```
(11)
```
  0.12
- 0.06
------
  0.06
```
(12)
```
  0.016
- 0.010
------
  0.006
```
(13)
```
  1.8
- 0.1
-----
  1.7
```
(14)
```
  0.14
- 0.01
------
  0.13
```
(15)
```
  0.009
- 0.008
------
  0.001
```
(16)
```
  1.8
- 0.5
-----
  1.3
```

(17)
```
  0.18
- 0.09
------
  0.09
```
(18)
```
  0.08
- 0.06
------
  0.02
```
(19)
```
  1.9
- 1.1
-----
  0.8
```
(20)
```
  0.15
- 0.07
------
  0.08
```
(21)
```
  0.12
- 0.04
------
  0.08
```
(22)
```
  1.2
- 0.5
-----
  0.7
```
(23)
```
  0.012
- 0.002
------
  0.010
```
(24)
```
  0.011
- 0.006
------
  0.005
```

(25)
```
  1.5
- 0.5
-----
  1.0
```
(26)
```
  0.19
- 0.12
------
  0.07
```
(27)
```
  1.1
- 0.2
-----
  0.9
```
(28)
```
  0.17
- 0.03
------
  0.14
```
(29)
```
  0.18
- 0.14
------
  0.04
```
(30)
```
  0.7
- 0.4
-----
  0.3
```

Page 51

① 13.9 − 6.2 = 7.7
② 0.091 − 0.006 = 0.085
③ 0.180 − 0.158 = 0.022
④ 1.60 − 0.41 = 1.19
⑤ 0.98 − 0.72 = 0.26
⑥ 15.8 − 5.0 = 10.8
⑦ 0.165 − 0.024 = 0.141
⑧ 1.74 − 0.05 = 1.69
⑨ 1.20 − 0.69 = 0.51

⑩ 13.3 − 11.0 = 2.3
⑪ 19.8 − 5.3 = 14.5
⑫ 1.19 − 1.14 = 0.05
⑬ 0.117 − 0.038 = 0.079
⑭ 0.195 − 0.003 = 0.192
⑮ 0.180 − 0.143 = 0.037
⑯ 1.78 − 0.54 = 1.24
⑰ 1.49 − 1.13 = 0.36
⑱ 17.2 − 2.5 = 14.7

⑲ 14.4 − 12.9 = 1.5
⑳ 1.81 − 1.81 = 0.00

Page 52

① 4.9 − 4.6 = 0.3
② 0.97 − 0.20 = 0.77
③ 0.11 − 0.09 = 0.02
④ 9.9 − 3.3 = 6.6
⑤ 6.0 − 4.8 = 1.2
⑥ 0.97 − 0.03 = 0.94
⑦ 9.5 − 6.9 = 2.6
⑧ 6.5 − 1.9 = 4.6
⑨ 0.41 − 0.18 = 0.23

⑩ 0.99 − 0.40 = 0.59
⑪ 2.1 − 2.1 = 0.0
⑫ 9.8 − 9.8 = 0.0
⑬ 0.68 − 0.21 = 0.47
⑭ 2.3 − 1.8 = 0.5
⑮ 0.75 − 0.56 = 0.19
⑯ 0.36 − 0.14 = 0.22
⑰ 0.65 − 0.22 = 0.43
⑱ 0.82 − 0.45 = 0.37

⑲ 0.33 − 0.23 = 0.10
⑳ 0.37 − 0.16 = 0.21
㉑ 4.2 − 0.2 = 4.0
㉒ 0.82 − 0.75 = 0.07
㉓ 7.1 − 5.9 = 1.2
㉔ 6.8 − 2.9 = 3.9
㉕ 5.0 − 2.5 = 2.5
㉖ 5.3 − 2.5 = 2.8
㉗ 4.3 − 1.7 = 2.6

㉘ 0.74 − 0.54 = 0.20
㉙ 9.5 − 6.1 = 3.4
㉚ 8.8 − 7.6 = 1.2

Page 53

① 8 × 0.4 = 3.2
② 4 × 0.5 = 2.0
③ 9 × 0.1 = 0.9
④ 4 × 0.7 = 2.8
⑤ 1 × 3.7 = 3.7
⑥ 3 × 2.7 = 8.1
⑦ 7 × 0.6 = 4.2
⑧ 2 × 4.3 = 8.6
⑨ 3 × 4.0 = 12.0

⑩ 6 × 4.4 = 26.4
⑪ 1 × 1.1 = 1.1
⑫ 9 × 5.5 = 49.5
⑬ 9 × 0.6 = 5.4
⑭ 8 × 0.6 = 4.8
⑮ 7 × 7.8 = 54.6
⑯ 4 × 0.2 = 0.8
⑰ 7 × 0.2 = 1.4
⑱ 6 × 0.4 = 2.4

⑲ 5 × 0.6 = 3.0
⑳ 6 × 8.1 = 48.6

Page 54

① 2 × 3.8 = 7.6
② 4 × 0.4 = 1.6
③ 2 × 8.6 = 17.2
④ 5 × 5.4 = 27.0
⑤ 7 × 0.2 = 1.4
⑥ 1 × 7.9 = 7.9
⑦ 6 × 0.1 = 0.6
⑧ 4 × 0.6 = 2.4
⑨ 4 × 5.6 = 22.4

⑩ 1 × 6.8 = 6.8
⑪ 1 × 2.7 = 2.7
⑫ 3 × 0.2 = 0.6
⑬ 1 × 4.1 = 4.1
⑭ 8 × 1.3 = 10.4
⑮ 7 × 1.5 = 10.5
⑯ 9 × 8.6 = 77.4
⑰ 3 × 0.8 = 2.4
⑱ 3 × 0.5 = 1.5

⑲ 6 × 3.4 = 20.4
⑳ 6 × 1.8 = 10.8
㉑ 2 × 7.0 = 14.0
㉒ 1 × 8.0 = 8.0
㉓ 5 × 0.5 = 2.5
㉔ 7 × 4.6 = 32.2
㉕ 7 × 8.9 = 62.3
㉖ 6 × 0.3 = 1.8
㉗ 3 × 1.6 = 4.8

㉘ 6 × 6.1 = 36.6
㉙ 8 × 7.3 = 58.4
㉚ 8 × 0.6 = 4.8

Page 55

(1)	(2)	(3)	(4)	(5)	(6)	(7)	(8)	(9)
3 × 4.7 — 14.1	3 × 3.5 — 10.5	3 × 0.3 — 0.9	4 × 3.5 — 14.0	2 × 1.9 — 3.8	4 × 1.4 — 5.6	8 × 0.5 — 4.0	4 × 0.7 — 2.8	6 × 0.0 — 0.0

(10)	(11)	(12)	(13)	(14)	(15)	(16)	(17)	(18)
5 × 0.8 — 4.0	3 × 0.7 — 2.1	3 × 3.8 — 11.4	6 × 0.8 — 4.8	3 × 1.3 — 3.9	8 × 6.5 — 52.0	4 × 3.1 — 12.4	3 × 7.2 — 21.6	7 × 0.0 — 0.0

(19)	(20)
1 × 7.5 — 7.5	1 × 0.4 — 0.4

Page 56

(1)	(2)	(3)	(4)	(5)	(6)	(7)	(8)	(9)
2 × 0.0 — 0.0	6 × 3.6 — 21.6	9 × 7.5 — 67.5	4 × 0.0 — 0.0	4 × 3.6 — 14.4	6 × 0.7 — 4.2	9 × 0.1 — 0.9	8 × 0.6 — 4.8	4 × 2.9 — 11.6

(10)	(11)	(12)	(13)	(14)	(15)	(16)	(17)	(18)
9 × 0.8 — 7.2	1 × 3.4 — 3.4	5 × 0.8 — 4.0	4 × 8.1 — 32.4	1 × 0.1 — 0.1	5 × 0.6 — 3.0	5 × 0.3 — 1.5	8 × 0.5 — 4.0	8 × 5.6 — 44.8

(19)	(20)	(21)	(22)	(23)	(24)	(25)	(26)	(27)
1 × 0.4 — 0.4	4 × 6.9 — 27.6	4 × 5.3 — 21.2	5 × 0.4 — 2.0	4 × 8.5 — 34.0	5 × 6.6 — 33.0	9 × 1.5 — 13.5	6 × 0.8 — 4.8	5 × 0.2 — 1.0

(28)	(29)	(30)
6 × 0.1 — 0.6	6 × 1.2 — 7.2	9 × 3.8 — 34.2

Page 57

(1)	(2)	(3)	(4)	(5)	(6)	(7)	(8)	(9)
0.31 × 1.0 — 0.310	9.2 × 0.16 — 1.472	1.1 × 65 — 71.5	36 × 0.69 — 24.84	34 × 9.5 — 323.0	76 × 69 — 5,244	0.73 × 100 — 73.00	1.6 × 28 — 44.8	0.70 × 0.05 — 0.0350

(10)	(11)	(12)	(13)	(14)	(15)	(16)	(17)	(18)
0.2 × 11 — 2.2	21 × 0.83 — 17.43	0.7 × 5.7 — 3.99	0.45 × 0.55 — 0.2475	5 × 0.59 — 2.95	0.73 × 6.0 — 4.380	0.56 × 3.0 — 1.680	35 × 67 — 2,345	26 × 1.4 — 36.4

(19)	(20)
49 × 7.0 — 343.0	0.84 × 60 — 50.40

Page 58

(1)	(2)	(3)	(4)	(5)	(6)	(7)	(8)	(9)
0.47 × 22 — 10.34	1 × 0.57 — 0.57	3.7 × 80 — 296.0	1 × 0.28 — 0.28	84 × 0.23 — 19.32	0.2 × 8.0 — 1.60	6.8 × 0.57 — 3.876	0.02 × 9.9 — 0.198	0.59 × 9 — 5.31

(10)	(11)	(12)	(13)	(14)	(15)	(16)	(17)	(18)
90 × 22 — 1,980	74 × 0.66 — 48.84	43 × 0.76 — 32.68	1.2 × 25 — 30.0	6 × 1.7 — 10.2	0.19 × 0.20 — 0.0380	49 × 0.19 — 9.31	5.2 × 28 — 145.6	0.90 × 72 — 64.80

(19)	(20)	(21)	(22)	(23)	(24)	(25)	(26)	(27)
4 × 67 — 268	54 × 0.47 — 25.38	0.64 × 87 — 55.68	4.8 × 5.0 — 24.00	4.6 × 1.9 — 8.74	38 × 0.62 — 23.56	0.97 × 4.9 — 4.753	5.7 × 1.4 — 7.98	0.64 × 0.99 — 0.6336

(28)	(29)	(30)
3.6 × 8.1 — 29.16	79 × 0.25 — 19.75	0.46 × 13 — 5.98

Answer Key   Grades 5-8

Page 59

(1)
$$\begin{array}{r} 8 \\ \times\ 24 \\ \hline 192 \end{array}$$

(2)
$$\begin{array}{r} 29 \\ \times\ 2.5 \\ \hline 72.5 \end{array}$$

(3)
$$\begin{array}{r} 0.98 \\ \times\ 1.2 \\ \hline 1.176 \end{array}$$

(4)
$$\begin{array}{r} 0.82 \\ \times\ 0.49 \\ \hline 0.4018 \end{array}$$

(5)
$$\begin{array}{r} 1.7 \\ \times\ 0.73 \\ \hline 1.241 \end{array}$$

(6)
$$\begin{array}{r} 56 \\ \times\ 0.62 \\ \hline 34.72 \end{array}$$

(7)
$$\begin{array}{r} 55 \\ \times\ 66 \\ \hline 3{,}630 \end{array}$$

(8)
$$\begin{array}{r} 27 \\ \times\ 0.31 \\ \hline 8.37 \end{array}$$

(9)
$$\begin{array}{r} 5.7 \\ \times\ 0.25 \\ \hline 1.425 \end{array}$$

(10)
$$\begin{array}{r} 6.4 \\ \times\ 0.57 \\ \hline 3.648 \end{array}$$

(11)
$$\begin{array}{r} 5.2 \\ \times\ 0.04 \\ \hline 0.208 \end{array}$$

(12)
$$\begin{array}{r} 4.1 \\ \times\ 1.5 \\ \hline 6.15 \end{array}$$

(13)
$$\begin{array}{r} 82 \\ \times\ 0.32 \\ \hline 26.24 \end{array}$$

(14)
$$\begin{array}{r} 0.91 \\ \times\ 0.15 \\ \hline 0.1365 \end{array}$$

(15)
$$\begin{array}{r} 79 \\ \times\ 56 \\ \hline 4{,}424 \end{array}$$

(16)
$$\begin{array}{r} 44 \\ \times\ 49 \\ \hline 2{,}156 \end{array}$$

(17)
$$\begin{array}{r} 3.4 \\ \times\ 6.0 \\ \hline 20.40 \end{array}$$

(18)
$$\begin{array}{r} 75 \\ \times\ 8.5 \\ \hline 637.5 \end{array}$$

(19)
$$\begin{array}{r} 15 \\ \times\ 1.2 \\ \hline 18.0 \end{array}$$

(20)
$$\begin{array}{r} 0.38 \\ \times\ 8.8 \\ \hline 3.344 \end{array}$$

Page 60

(1)
$$\begin{array}{r} 68 \\ \times\ 83 \\ \hline 5{,}644 \end{array}$$

(2)
$$\begin{array}{r} 44 \\ \times\ 42 \\ \hline 1{,}848 \end{array}$$

(3)
$$\begin{array}{r} 0.91 \\ \times\ 6.4 \\ \hline 5.824 \end{array}$$

(4)
$$\begin{array}{r} 37 \\ \times\ 3.0 \\ \hline 111.0 \end{array}$$

(5)
$$\begin{array}{r} 0.05 \\ \times\ 0.91 \\ \hline 0.0455 \end{array}$$

(6)
$$\begin{array}{r} 4 \\ \times\ 0.50 \\ \hline 2.00 \end{array}$$

(7)
$$\begin{array}{r} 0.27 \\ \times\ 7.8 \\ \hline 2.106 \end{array}$$

(8)
$$\begin{array}{r} 0.32 \\ \times\ 94 \\ \hline 30.08 \end{array}$$

(9)
$$\begin{array}{r} 4 \\ \times\ 8.2 \\ \hline 32.8 \end{array}$$

(10)
$$\begin{array}{r} 0.68 \\ \times\ 2.7 \\ \hline 1.836 \end{array}$$

(11)
$$\begin{array}{r} 3.5 \\ \times\ 83 \\ \hline 290.5 \end{array}$$

(12)
$$\begin{array}{r} 75 \\ \times\ 0.54 \\ \hline 40.50 \end{array}$$

(13)
$$\begin{array}{r} 60 \\ \times\ 0.59 \\ \hline 35.40 \end{array}$$

(14)
$$\begin{array}{r} 9 \\ \times\ 0.90 \\ \hline 8.10 \end{array}$$

(15)
$$\begin{array}{r} 0.36 \\ \times\ 0.72 \\ \hline 0.2592 \end{array}$$

(16)
$$\begin{array}{r} 0.19 \\ \times\ 0.85 \\ \hline 0.1615 \end{array}$$

(17)
$$\begin{array}{r} 0.48 \\ \times\ 9.5 \\ \hline 4.560 \end{array}$$

(18)
$$\begin{array}{r} 3.5 \\ \times\ 0.14 \\ \hline 0.490 \end{array}$$

(19)
$$\begin{array}{r} 0.92 \\ \times\ 5.6 \\ \hline 5.152 \end{array}$$

(20)
$$\begin{array}{r} 0.84 \\ \times\ 17 \\ \hline 14.28 \end{array}$$

(21)
$$\begin{array}{r} 4 \\ \times\ 0.97 \\ \hline 3.88 \end{array}$$

(22)
$$\begin{array}{r} 7.1 \\ \times\ 0.96 \\ \hline 6.816 \end{array}$$

(23)
$$\begin{array}{r} 55 \\ \times\ 2.3 \\ \hline 126.5 \end{array}$$

(24)
$$\begin{array}{r} 5.4 \\ \times\ 15 \\ \hline 81.0 \end{array}$$

(25)
$$\begin{array}{r} 9.4 \\ \times\ 96 \\ \hline 902.4 \end{array}$$

(26)
$$\begin{array}{r} 45 \\ \times\ 0.79 \\ \hline 35.55 \end{array}$$

(27)
$$\begin{array}{r} 0.10 \\ \times\ 6.3 \\ \hline 0.630 \end{array}$$

(28)
$$\begin{array}{r} 0.08 \\ \times\ 8.4 \\ \hline 0.672 \end{array}$$

(29)
$$\begin{array}{r} 1.0 \\ \times\ 0.90 \\ \hline 0.900 \end{array}$$

(30)
$$\begin{array}{r} 8.2 \\ \times\ 33 \\ \hline 270.6 \end{array}$$

Page 61

(1) $9\overline{)8.56} = 0.951$
(2) $2\overline{)5.19} = 2.595$
(3) $5\overline{)0.44} = 0.088$
(4) $5\overline{)6.87} = 1.374$
(5) $1\overline{)0.24} = 0.24$
(6) $1\overline{)5.44} = 5.44$
(7) $6\overline{)0.86} = 0.143$

(8) $8\overline{)0.23} = 0.029$
(9) $4\overline{)9.02} = 2.255$
(10) $7\overline{)9.13} = 1.304$
(11) $7\overline{)8.72} = 1.246$
(12) $7\overline{)3.84} = 0.549$
(13) $7\overline{)0.92} = 0.131$
(14) $5\overline{)6.80} = 1.36$

(15) $6\overline{)0.51} = 0.085$
(16) $4\overline{)0.64} = 0.16$
(17) $9\overline{)8.45} = 0.939$
(18) $8\overline{)2.79} = 0.349$
(19) $8\overline{)7.71} = 0.964$
(20) $4\overline{)4.08} = 1.02$

Page 62

(1) $2\overline{)8.77} = 4.385$
(2) $8\overline{)8.46} = 1.058$
(3) $6\overline{)9.17} = 1.528$
(4) $4\overline{)7.09} = 1.773$
(5) $3\overline{)8.55} = 2.85$
(6) $5\overline{)7.26} = 1.452$
(7) $9\overline{)8.29} = 0.921$

(8) $4\overline{)8.37} = 2.093$
(9) $4\overline{)0.38} = 0.095$
(10) $7\overline{)0.75} = 0.107$
(11) $5\overline{)9.64} = 1.928$
(12) $8\overline{)3.17} = 0.396$
(13) $10\overline{)2.66} = 0.266$
(14) $3\overline{)0.66} = 0.22$

(15) $9\overline{)4.88} = 0.542$
(16) $4\overline{)8.04} = 2.01$
(17) $5\overline{)5.19} = 1.038$
(18) $6\overline{)9.72} = 1.62$
(19) $6\overline{)0.04} = 0.007$
(20) $2\overline{)9.28} = 4.64$
(21) $2\overline{)0.12} = 0.06$

(22) $3\overline{)2.31} = 0.77$
(23) $5\overline{)0.37} = 0.074$
(24) $4\overline{)3.72} = 0.93$
(25) $7\overline{)0.65} = 0.093$
(26) $6\overline{)2.87} = 0.478$
(27) $5\overline{)9.11} = 1.822$
(28) $5\overline{)0.44} = 0.088$

(29) $2\overline{)8.19} = 4.095$
(30) $9\overline{)5.71} = 0.634$

Page 63

(1) $3\overline{)0.25} = 0.083$
(2) $8\overline{)6.25} = 0.781$
(3) $1\overline{)2.36} = 2.36$
(4) $5\overline{)5.08} = 1.016$
(5) $6\overline{)0.26} = 0.043$
(6) $7\overline{)8.52} = 1.217$
(7) $1\overline{)5.27} = 5.27$

(8) $4\overline{)1.54} = 0.385$
(9) $3\overline{)0.58} = 0.193$
(10) $4\overline{)9.46} = 2.365$
(11) $6\overline{)2.89} = 0.482$
(12) $6\overline{)0.11} = 0.018$
(13) $3\overline{)0.62} = 0.207$
(14) $4\overline{)2.24} = 0.56$

(15) $9\overline{)0.31} = 0.034$
(16) $2\overline{)0.74} = 0.37$
(17) $3\overline{)0.04} = 0.013$
(18) $5\overline{)3.45} = 0.69$
(19) $8\overline{)1.35} = 0.169$
(20) $9\overline{)8.59} = 0.954$

Page 64

(1) $5\overline{)0.67}$ = 0.134 (2) $2\overline{)7.56}$ = 3.78 (3) $7\overline{)0.24}$ = 0.034 (4) $6\overline{)9.87}$ = 1.645 (5) $8\overline{)0.35}$ = 0.044 (6) $8\overline{)7.34}$ = 0.918 (7) $4\overline{)0.92}$ = 0.23

(8) $9\overline{)0.41}$ = 0.046 (9) $9\overline{)4.38}$ = 0.487 (10) $8\overline{)5.12}$ = 0.64 (11) $1\overline{)5.33}$ = 5.33 (12) $2\overline{)6.34}$ = 3.17 (13) $7\overline{)8.23}$ = 1.176 (14) $10\overline{)0.73}$ = 0.073

(15) $5\overline{)0.29}$ = 0.058 (16) $2\overline{)8.56}$ = 4.28 (17) $5\overline{)1.58}$ = 0.316 (18) $7\overline{)85}$ = 12.143 (19) $6\overline{)0.30}$ = 0.05 (20) $2\overline{)2.30}$ = 1.15 (21) $5\overline{)8.88}$ = 1.776

(22) $7\overline{)7.66}$ = 1.094 (23) $5\overline{)5.65}$ = 1.13 (24) $3\overline{)0.41}$ = 0.137 (25) $1\overline{)1.22}$ = 1.22 (26) $6\overline{)0.21}$ = 0.035 (27) $4\overline{)8.43}$ = 2.108 (28) $7\overline{)4.06}$ = 0.58

(29) $7\overline{)8.82}$ = 1.26 (30) $6\overline{)0.34}$ = 0.057

Page 65

(1) $3.6\overline{)0.12}$ = 0.033 (2) $22.7\overline{)5.1}$ = 0.225 (3) $85.0\overline{)1.6}$ = 0.019 (4) $6.93\overline{)0.48}$ = 0.069 (5) $9.96\overline{)0.02}$ = 0.002 (6) $35.2\overline{)0.89}$ = 0.025

(7) $10.3\overline{)0.65}$ = 0.063 (8) $5.20\overline{)1.0}$ = 0.192 (9) $2.20\overline{)0.90}$ = 0.409 (10) $63.2\overline{)6.69}$ = 0.106 (11) $4.76\overline{)1.06}$ = 0.223 (12) $3.26\overline{)8.7}$ = 2.669

(13) $4.22\overline{)0.22}$ = 0.052 (14) $50.9\overline{)0.97}$ = 0.019 (15) $0.31\overline{)0.100}$ = 0.323 (16) $3.06\overline{)0.1}$ = 0.033 (17) $45.5\overline{)5.1}$ = 0.112 (18) $0.41\overline{)0.014}$ = 0.034

(19) $4.80\overline{)8.2}$ = 1.708 (20) $1.13\overline{)0.019}$ = 0.017

Page 66

(1) $2.63\overline{)7.1}$ = 2.700 (2) $85.9\overline{)0.057}$ = 0.001 (3) $25.5\overline{)0.036}$ = 0.001 (4) $8.89\overline{)0.071}$ = 0.008 (5) $88.2\overline{)0.002}$ = 0.000 (6) $8.37\overline{)16}$ = 1.912

(7) $0.56\overline{)0.50}$ = 0.893 (8) $3.06\overline{)9.2}$ = 3.007 (9) $8.17\overline{)0.93}$ = 0.114 (10) $2.99\overline{)0.046}$ = 0.015 (11) $70.5\overline{)0.59}$ = 0.008 (12) $5.04\overline{)0.48}$ = 0.095

(13) $2.17\overline{)1.2}$ = 0.553 (14) $7.30\overline{)0.024}$ = 0.003 (15) $59.0\overline{)0.013}$ = 0.000 (16) $4.86\overline{)3.7}$ = 0.761 (17) $6.06\overline{)6.2}$ = 1.023 (18) $8.55\overline{)1.2}$ = 0.140

(19) $2.27\overline{)0.76}$ = 0.335 (20) $89.6\overline{)8.9}$ = 0.099 (21) $6.19\overline{)0.036}$ = 0.006 (22) $7.29\overline{)0.013}$ = 0.002 (23) $26.4\overline{)0.075}$ = 0.003 (24) $73.5\overline{)5.4}$ = 0.073

(25) $7.8\overline{)0.02}$ = 0.003 (26) $9.24\overline{)0.014}$ = 0.002 (27) $3.77\overline{)8.1}$ = 2.149 (28) $6.39\overline{)0.47}$ = 0.074 (29) $6.2\overline{)0.78}$ = 0.126 (30) $14.3\overline{)0.074}$ = 0.005

Page 67

(1) $65.5\overline{)0.92}$ = 0.014 (2) $5.75\overline{)0.60}$ = 0.104 (3) $62.9\overline{)0.84}$ = 0.013 (4) $3.82\overline{)0.83}$ = 0.217 (5) $49.7\overline{)0.59}$ = 0.012 (6) $8.56\overline{)0.051}$ = 0.006 (7) $6.05\overline{)5.56}$ = 0.919

(8) $14.8\overline{)4.7}$ = 0.318 (9) $9.95\overline{)3.02}$ = 0.304 (10) $8.56\overline{)0.46}$ = 0.054 (11) $8.87\overline{)0.81}$ = 0.091 (12) $9.51\overline{)6.8}$ = 0.715 (13) $10.6\overline{)0.024}$ = 0.002 (14) $12.1\overline{)0.78}$ = 0.064

(15) $1.001\overline{)9.0}$ = 8.99 (16) $87.8\overline{)0.001}$ = 0.000 (17) $59.0\overline{)0.048}$ = 0.001 (18) $3.16\overline{)0.92}$ = 0.291 (19) $2.55\overline{)1.8}$ = 0.706 (20) $2.32\overline{)0.022}$ = 0.009

Page 68

(1) $1.68\overline{)8.7}$ = 5.179 (2) $3.8\overline{)3.02}$ = 0.795 (3) $27.4\overline{)1.59}$ = 0.058 (4) $2.90\overline{)0.031}$ = 0.011 (5) $18.4\overline{)7.9}$ = 0.429 (6) $0.77\overline{)8.1}$ = 10.519

(7) $0.3\overline{)1.7}$ = 5.667 (8) $8.3\overline{)5.5}$ = 0.663 (9) $8.5\overline{)51}$ = 6 (10) $0.24\overline{)5.3}$ = 22.083 (11) $2.28\overline{)2.50}$ = 1.096 (12) $1.02\overline{)0.061}$ = 0.060

(13) $1.53\overline{)0.95}$ = 0.621 (14) $1.48\overline{)8.8}$ = 5.946 (15) $8.7\overline{)9.5}$ = 1.092 (16) $29.8\overline{)1.6}$ = 0.054 (17) $2.15\overline{)8.5}$ = 3.953 (18) $2.13\overline{)0.083}$ = 0.039

(19) $22.6\overline{)9.6}$ = 0.425 (20) $5.9\overline{)9.3}$ = 1.576 (21) $27.8\overline{)0.025}$ = 0.001 (22) $17.7\overline{)0.050}$ = 0.003 (23) $15.5\overline{)6.1}$ = 0.394 (24) $15.4\overline{)0.79}$ = 0.051

(25) $7.1\overline{)0.78}$ = 0.110 (26) $2.58\overline{)3.2}$ = 1.240 (27) $10.3\overline{)8.05}$ = 0.782 (28) $6.2\overline{)0.79}$ = 0.127 (29) $33.2\overline{)0.089}$ = 0.003 (30) $24.5\overline{)0.16}$ = 0.007

Page 69

(1) $0.389 = 38\frac{9}{10}\%$ (2) $0.56 = 56\%$ (3) $0.147 = 14\frac{7}{10}\%$ (4) $0.198 = 19\frac{4}{5}\%$ (5) $0.45 = 45\%$

(6) $0.445 = 44\frac{1}{2}\%$ (7) $0.472 = 47\frac{1}{4}\%$ (8) $0.435 = 43\frac{1}{2}\%$ (9) $0.913 = 91\frac{3}{10}\%$ (10) $0.05 = 5\%$

(11) $0.688 = 68\frac{3}{4}\%$ (12) $0.558 = 55\frac{4}{5}\%$ (13) $0.458 = 45\frac{8}{10}\%$ (14) $0.665 = 66\frac{1}{2}\%$ (15) $0.942 = 94\frac{1}{4}\%$

(16) $0.97 = 97\%$ (17) $0.212 = 21\frac{1}{5}\%$ (18) $0.557 = 55\frac{7}{10}\%$ (19) $0.134 = 13\frac{2}{5}\%$ (20) $0.48 = 48\%$

(21) $0.075 = 7\frac{2}{4}\%$ (22) $0.075 = 7\frac{1}{2}\%$ (23) $0.895 = 89\frac{1}{2}\%$ (24) $0.41 = 41\%$ (25) $0.855 = 85\frac{2}{4}\%$

Page 70

(1) $84\frac{1}{4}\% = 0.842$ (2) $1\frac{4}{5}\% = 0.018$ (3) $18\% = 0.18$ (4) $31\frac{5}{10}\% = 0.315$ (5) $90\frac{1}{4}\% = 0.902$

(6) $55\frac{2}{5}\% = 0.554$ (7) $51\frac{1}{2}\% = 0.515$ (8) $66\% = 0.66$ (9) $57\frac{3}{5}\% = 0.576$ (10) $74\frac{1}{2}\% = 0.745$

(11) $74\frac{1}{10}\% = 0.741$ (12) $67\frac{1}{4}\% = 0.672$ (13) $93\% = 0.93$ (14) $60\frac{2}{4}\% = 0.605$ (15) $63\frac{3}{5}\% = 0.636$

(16) $70\frac{4}{10}\% = 0.704$ (17) $42\frac{1}{2}\% = 0.425$ (18) $51\frac{1}{4}\% = 0.512$ (19) $49\frac{1}{2}\% = 0.495$ (20) $52\frac{3}{10}\% = 0.523$

(21) $60\frac{1}{5}\% = 0.602$ (22) $6\% = 0.06$ (23) $70\frac{6}{10}\% = 0.706$ (24) $58\% = 0.58$ (25) $47\frac{1}{2}\% = 0.475$

Page 71

(1) $0.821 = 82\frac{1}{10}\%$ (2) $1 = 100\%$ (3) $0.155 = 15\frac{1}{2}\%$ (4) $0.477 = 47\frac{2}{3}\%$ (5) $0.32 = 32\%$

(6) $0.965 = 96\frac{1}{2}\%$ (7) $0.099 = 9\frac{9}{10}\%$ (8) $0.864 = 86\frac{2}{5}\%$ (9) $0.238 = 23\frac{3}{4}\%$ (10) $0.04 = 4\%$

(11) $0.412 = 41\frac{1}{4}\%$ (12) $0.365 = 36\frac{5}{10}\%$ (13) $0.393 = 39\frac{1}{3}\%$ (14) $0.075 = 7\frac{1}{2}\%$ (15) $0.838 = 83\frac{4}{5}\%$

(16) $0.734 = 73\frac{2}{5}\%$ (17) $0.932 = 93\frac{1}{4}\%$ (18) $0.637 = 63\frac{2}{3}\%$ (19) $0.408 = 40\frac{8}{10}\%$ (20) $0.01 = 1\%$

(21) $0.125 = 12\frac{1}{2}\%$ (22) $0.895 = 89\frac{2}{4}\%$ (23) $0.67 = 67\%$ (24) $0.465 = 46\frac{1}{2}\%$ (25) $0.303 = 30\frac{1}{3}\%$

Page 72

(1) $8\frac{4}{5}\% = 0.088$ (2) $87\frac{5}{10}\% = 0.875$ (3) $41\% = 0.41$ (4) $62\frac{4}{10}\% = 0.624$ (5) $30\frac{1}{2}\% = 0.305$

(6) $72\frac{3}{4}\% = 0.728$ (7) $3\frac{1}{3}\% = 0.033$ (8) $93\frac{2}{5}\% = 0.934$ (9) $81\frac{2}{3}\% = 0.817$ (10) $38\frac{1}{5}\% = 0.382$

(11) $91\frac{9}{10}\% = 0.919$ (12) $92\frac{1}{2}\% = 0.925$ (13) $43\frac{2}{4}\% = 0.435$ (14) $26\% = 0.26$ (15) $44\frac{1}{4}\% = 0.442$

(16) $82\frac{1}{2}\% = 0.825$ (17) $47\frac{3}{10}\% = 0.473$ (18) $78\frac{2}{3}\% = 0.787$ (19) $7\% = 0.07$ (20) $20\% = 0.2$

(21) $75\frac{4}{5}\% = 0.758$ (22) $66\frac{4}{10}\% = 0.664$ (23) $33\frac{2}{3}\% = 0.337$ (24) $53\frac{1}{4}\% = 0.532$ (25) $1\frac{1}{2}\% = 0.015$

Page 73

(1) $4.9 \times 0.02 = 0.098$
(2) $0.71 \times 0.002 = 0.00142$
(3) $2.4 \times 1.000 = 2.4$
(4) $6.6 \times 9.000 = 59.4$
(5) $9.05 \times 3.00 = 27.15$
(6) $7.4 \times 8.00 = 59.2$
(7) $0.16 \times 0.004 = 0.00064$
(8) $9.5 \times 6.0 = 57.0$
(9) $0.70 \times 0.2 = 0.140$

(10) $7.4 \times 6.000 = 44.4$
(11) $0.84 \times 0.003 = 0.00252$
(12) $3.2 \times 4.0 = 12.8$
(13) $0.57 \times 0.006 = 0.00342$
(14) $3.6 \times 9.000 = 32.4$
(15) $6.7 \times 0.04 = 0.268$
(16) $0.45 \times 0.2 = 0.090$
(17) $0.34 \times 0.004 = 0.00136$
(18) $2.4 \times 2.00 = 4.8$

(19) $8.5 \times 0.07 = 0.595$
(20) $0.74 \times 0.3 = 0.222$

Page 74

(1) $0.72 \times 0.8 = 0.576$
(2) $7.0 \times 0.1 = 0.70$
(3) $84 \times 0.6 = 50.4$
(4) $90 \times 0.5 = 45.0$
(5) $63 \times 0.005 = 0.315$
(6) $5.8 \times 8.000 = 46.4$
(7) $1.5 \times 5.00 = 7.5$
(8) $1.07 \times 2.00 = 2.14$
(9) $5.2 \times 0.006 = 0.0312$

(10) $8.05 \times 4.0 = 32.20$
(11) $4.6 \times 3.0 = 13.8$
(12) $0.63 \times 0.001 = 0.00063$
(13) $8.6 \times 7.000 = 60.2$
(14) $0.65 \times 0.2 = 0.130$
(15) $3.9 \times 4.000 = 15.6$
(16) $0.29 \times 0.006 = 0.00174$
(17) $0.21 \times 0.8 = 0.168$
(18) $5.9 \times 0.5 = 2.95$

(19) $9.01 \times 8.0 = 72.08$
(20) $7.7 \times 8.0 = 61.6$
(21) $1.6 \times 1.00 = 1.6$
(22) $0.18 \times 0.2 = 0.036$
(23) $2.7 \times 9.00 = 24.3$
(24) $0.24 \times 0.001 = 0.00024$
(25) $0.28 \times 0.4 = 0.112$
(26) $0.25 \times 0.07 = 0.0175$
(27) $0.62 \times 0.02 = 0.0124$

(28) $7.3 \times 9.000 = 65.7$
(29) $8.7 \times 2.0 = 17.4$
(30) $5.7 \times 4.0 = 22.8$

Answer Key

Page 75

1. 4.1 × 0.01 = 0.041
2. 9.7 × 0.1 = 0.97
3. 9.5 × 1.00 = 9.5
4. 0.73 × 0.01 = 0.0073
5. 0.92 × 0.1 = 0.092
6. 0.89 × 0.1 = 0.089
7. 0.87 × 0.001 = 0.00087
8. 0.21 × 0.01 = 0.0021
9. 7.4 × 0.1 = 0.74
10. 3.5 × 1.000 = 3.5
11. 9.6 × 0.1 = 0.96
12. 0.15 × 0.01 = 0.0015
13. 0.81 × 0.01 = 0.0081
14. 6.3 × 0.1 = 0.63
15. 6.5 × 1.000 = 6.5
16. 4.8 × 1.00 = 4.8
17. 0.50 × 0.001 = 0.00050
18. 2.6 × 1.000 = 2.6
19. 5.7 × 1.00 = 5.7
20. 1.6 × 0.01 = 0.016

Page 76

1. 1.7 × 1.000 = 1.7
2. 0.42 × 0.1 = 0.042
3. 0.26 × 0.1 = 0.026
4. 5.6 × 1.000 = 5.6
5. 4.9 × 0.1 = 0.49
6. 1.1 × 0.001 = 0.0011
7. 0.67 × 0.01 = 0.0067
8. 2.3 × 1.00 = 2.3
9. 0.57 × 0.01 = 0.0057
10. 5.5 × 0.01 = 0.055
11. 2.0 × 0.1 = 0.20
12. 2.3 × 1.000 = 2.3
13. 0.46 × 0.01 = 0.0046
14. 5.5 × 1.0 = 5.5
15. 0.14 × 0.01 = 0.0014
16. 0.10 × 0.01 = 0.0010
17. 2.5 × 0.1 = 0.25
18. 2.4 × 1.000 = 2.4
19. 0.48 × 0.01 = 0.0048
20. 10.0 × 0.1 = 1.00
21. 2.8 × 0.1 = 0.28
22. 0.34 × 0.001 = 0.00034
23. 1.2 × 0.01 = 0.012
24. 0.28 × 0.1 = 0.028
25. 7.8 × 1.00 = 7.8
26. 6.14 × 1.000 = 6.14
27. 1.14 × 1.000 = 1.14
28. 5.4 × 0.001 = 0.0054
29. 8.2 × 1.0 = 8.2
30. 0.39 × 0.1 = 0.039

Page 77

1. 0.36 × 1,000 = 360.00
2. 6.3 × 100 = 630.0
3. 0.21 × 1,000 = 210.00
4. 9.95 × 100 = 995.00
5. 4.32 × 10 = 43.20
6. 2.2 × 10 = 22.0
7. 0.98 × 1,000 = 980.00
8. 0.67 × 100 = 67.00
9. 0.40 × 100 = 40.00
10. 3.33 × 10 = 33.30
11. 7.4 × 1,000 = 7,400.0
12. 7.5 × 100 = 750.0
13. 8.9 × 1,000 = 8,900.0
14. 0.75 × 1,000 = 750.00
15. 0.22 × 1,000 = 220.00
16. 0.62 × 1,000 = 620.00
17. 7.4 × 10 = 74.0
18. 4.4 × 10 = 44.0
19. 0.61 × 100 = 61.00
20. 3.6 × 10 = 36.0

Page 78

1. 0.47 × 100 = 47.00
2. 0.51 × 1,000 = 510.00
3. 5.6 × 10 = 56.0
4. 2.1 × 10 = 21.0
5. 7.02 × 100 = 702.00
6. 0.65 × 100 = 65.00
7. 0.80 × 1,000 = 800.00
8. 0.96 × 100 = 96.00
9. 8.5 × 10 = 85.0
10. 0.70 × 1,000 = 700.00
11. 1.45 × 10 = 14.50
12. 6.9 × 100 = 690.0
13. 9.401 × 10 = 94.010
14. 0.73 × 100 = 73.00
15. 8.9 × 1,000 = 8,900.0
16. 5.3 × 10 = 53.0
17. 2.35 × 1,000 = 2,350.00
18. 1.15 × 10 = 11.50
19. 4.9 × 10 = 49.0
20. 1.3 × 1,000 = 1,300.0
21. 9.5 × 100 = 950.0
22. 8.8 × 1,000 = 8,800.0
23. 0.50 × 100 = 50.00
24. 1.6 × 10 = 16.0
25. 0.44 × 10 = 4.40
26. 0.73 × 1,000 = 730.00
27. 7.9 × 1,000 = 7,900.0
28. 0.13 × 1,000 = 130.00
29. 4.7 × 1,000 = 4,700.0
30. 9.02 × 100 = 902.00

Page 79

1. 0.45 × 1,000 = 450.00
2. 4.4 × 100 = 440.0
3. 1.07 × 10 = 10.70
4. 5.2 × 100 = 520.0
5. 7.1 × 10 = 71.0
6. 0.61 × 10 = 6.10
7. 7.3 × 100 = 730.0
8. 0.33 × 10 = 3.30
9. 0.31 × 100 = 31.00
10. 0.59 × 1,000 = 590.00
11. 0.54 × 1,000 = 540.00
12. 9.1 × 100 = 910.0
13. 0.51 × 1,000 = 510.00
14. 0.75 × 1,000 = 750.00
15. 6.9 × 1,000 = 6,900.0
16. 0.70 × 100 = 70.00
17. 2.7 × 10 = 27.0
18. 0.41 × 10 = 4.10
19. 0.115 × 100 = 11.500
20. 4.6 × 1,000 = 4,600.0

Answer Key

Page 80

① $\begin{array}{r} 0.60 \\ \times\ \ 10 \\ \hline 6.00 \end{array}$ ② $\begin{array}{r} 4.7 \\ \times\ 100 \\ \hline 470.0 \end{array}$ ③ $\begin{array}{r} 0.78 \\ \times\ 1{,}000 \\ \hline 780.00 \end{array}$ ④ $\begin{array}{r} 0.65 \\ \times\ 100 \\ \hline 65.00 \end{array}$ ⑤ $\begin{array}{r} 0.27 \\ \times\ 100 \\ \hline 27.00 \end{array}$ ⑥ $\begin{array}{r} 4.0 \\ \times\ 10 \\ \hline 40.0 \end{array}$ ⑦ $\begin{array}{r} 0.45 \\ \times\ 10 \\ \hline 4.50 \end{array}$ ⑧ $\begin{array}{r} 9.2 \\ \times\ 1{,}000 \\ \hline 9{,}200.0 \end{array}$ ⑨ $\begin{array}{r} 6.4 \\ \times\ 1{,}000 \\ \hline 6{,}400.0 \end{array}$

⑩ $\begin{array}{r} 3.5 \\ \times\ 1{,}000 \\ \hline 3{,}500.0 \end{array}$ ⑪ $\begin{array}{r} 3.5 \\ \times\ 10 \\ \hline 35.0 \end{array}$ ⑫ $\begin{array}{r} 0.93 \\ \times\ 10 \\ \hline 9.30 \end{array}$ ⑬ $\begin{array}{r} 0.93 \\ \times\ 100 \\ \hline 93.00 \end{array}$ ⑭ $\begin{array}{r} 0.15 \\ \times\ 1{,}000 \\ \hline 150.00 \end{array}$ ⑮ $\begin{array}{r} 9.0 \\ \times\ 1{,}000 \\ \hline 9{,}000.0 \end{array}$ ⑯ $\begin{array}{r} 0.21 \\ \times\ 100 \\ \hline 21.00 \end{array}$ ⑰ $\begin{array}{r} 0.22 \\ \times\ 100 \\ \hline 22.00 \end{array}$ ⑱ $\begin{array}{r} 0.79 \\ \times\ 1{,}000 \\ \hline 790.00 \end{array}$

⑲ $\begin{array}{r} 6.8 \\ \times\ 100 \\ \hline 680.0 \end{array}$ ⑳ $\begin{array}{r} 0.81 \\ \times\ 10 \\ \hline 8.10 \end{array}$ ㉑ $\begin{array}{r} 10.11 \\ \times\ 100 \\ \hline 1{,}011.00 \end{array}$ ㉒ $\begin{array}{r} 8.9 \\ \times\ 10 \\ \hline 89.0 \end{array}$ ㉓ $\begin{array}{r} 25.3 \\ \times\ 100 \\ \hline 2{,}530.0 \end{array}$ ㉔ $\begin{array}{r} 6.72 \\ \times\ 10 \\ \hline 67.20 \end{array}$ ㉕ $\begin{array}{r} 3.9 \\ \times\ 10 \\ \hline 39.0 \end{array}$ ㉖ $\begin{array}{r} 1.4 \\ \times\ 100 \\ \hline 140.0 \end{array}$ ㉗ $\begin{array}{r} 48.5 \\ \times\ 1{,}000 \\ \hline 48{,}500.0 \end{array}$

㉘ $\begin{array}{r} 56.7 \\ \times\ 1{,}000 \\ \hline 56{,}700.0 \end{array}$ ㉙ $\begin{array}{r} 7.89 \\ \times\ 10 \\ \hline 78.90 \end{array}$ ㉚ $\begin{array}{r} 7.2 \\ \times\ 1{,}000 \\ \hline 7{,}200.0 \end{array}$

Page 81

① $\frac{1}{10}$ $1\frac{1}{10}$ $1\frac{2}{5}$ $\frac{2}{5}$ $\frac{4}{5}$

② $\frac{5}{8}$ $1\frac{1}{2}$ $\frac{1}{4}$ $1\frac{1}{8}$ $1\frac{7}{8}$

③ $1\frac{9}{10}$ $1\frac{1}{2}$ $\frac{3}{10}$ $1\frac{1}{5}$ $\frac{9}{10}$

④ $\frac{1}{8}$ $1\frac{1}{4}$ $1\frac{7}{8}$ $\frac{1}{2}$ $\frac{7}{8}$

⑤ $\frac{3}{8}$ $1\frac{1}{8}$ $\frac{3}{4}$ $1\frac{3}{4}$ $1\frac{1}{2}$

⑥ $\frac{3}{10}$ $1\frac{9}{10}$ 1 $\frac{7}{10}$ $1\frac{3}{5}$

⑦ $\frac{1}{2}$ $\frac{1}{5}$ $1\frac{3}{10}$ 1 $1\frac{9}{10}$

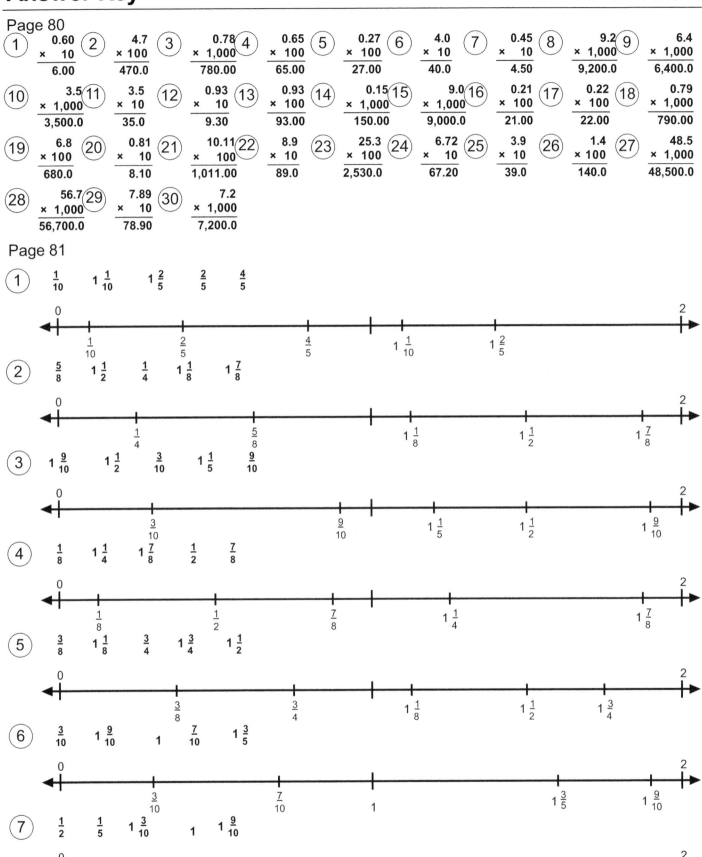

Answer Key

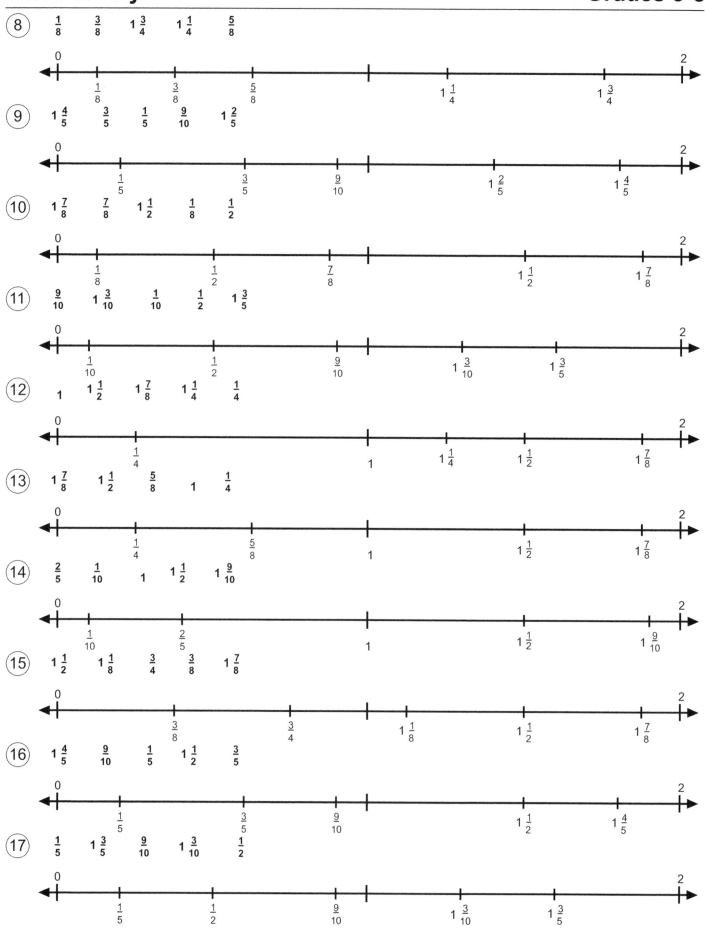

⑧ $\frac{1}{8}$ $\frac{3}{8}$ $1\frac{3}{4}$ $1\frac{1}{4}$ $\frac{5}{8}$

  0   2
  $\frac{1}{8}$ $\frac{3}{8}$ $\frac{5}{8}$ $1\frac{1}{4}$ $1\frac{3}{4}$

⑨ $1\frac{4}{5}$ $\frac{3}{5}$ $\frac{1}{5}$ $\frac{9}{10}$ $1\frac{2}{5}$

  0   2
  $\frac{1}{5}$ $\frac{3}{5}$ $\frac{9}{10}$ $1\frac{2}{5}$ $1\frac{4}{5}$

⑩ $1\frac{7}{8}$ $\frac{7}{8}$ $1\frac{1}{2}$ $\frac{1}{8}$ $\frac{1}{2}$

  0   2
  $\frac{1}{8}$ $\frac{1}{2}$ $\frac{7}{8}$ $1\frac{1}{2}$ $1\frac{7}{8}$

⑪ $\frac{9}{10}$ $1\frac{3}{10}$ $\frac{1}{10}$ $\frac{1}{2}$ $1\frac{3}{5}$

  0   2
  $\frac{1}{10}$ $\frac{1}{2}$ $\frac{9}{10}$ $1\frac{3}{10}$ $1\frac{3}{5}$

⑫ 1 $1\frac{1}{2}$ $1\frac{7}{8}$ $1\frac{1}{4}$ $\frac{1}{4}$

  0   2
  $\frac{1}{4}$ 1 $1\frac{1}{4}$ $1\frac{1}{2}$ $1\frac{7}{8}$

⑬ $1\frac{7}{8}$ $1\frac{1}{2}$ $\frac{5}{8}$ 1 $\frac{1}{4}$

  0   2
  $\frac{1}{4}$ $\frac{5}{8}$ 1 $1\frac{1}{2}$ $1\frac{7}{8}$

⑭ $\frac{2}{5}$ $\frac{1}{10}$ 1 $1\frac{1}{2}$ $1\frac{9}{10}$

  0   2
  $\frac{1}{10}$ $\frac{2}{5}$ 1 $1\frac{1}{2}$ $1\frac{9}{10}$

⑮ $1\frac{1}{2}$ $1\frac{1}{8}$ $\frac{3}{4}$ $\frac{3}{8}$ $1\frac{7}{8}$

  0   2
  $\frac{3}{8}$ $\frac{3}{4}$ $1\frac{1}{8}$ $1\frac{1}{2}$ $1\frac{7}{8}$

⑯ $1\frac{4}{5}$ $\frac{9}{10}$ $\frac{1}{5}$ $1\frac{1}{2}$ $\frac{3}{5}$

  0   2
  $\frac{1}{5}$ $\frac{3}{5}$ $\frac{9}{10}$ $1\frac{1}{2}$ $1\frac{4}{5}$

⑰ $\frac{1}{5}$ $1\frac{3}{5}$ $\frac{9}{10}$ $1\frac{3}{10}$ $\frac{1}{2}$

  0   2
  $\frac{1}{5}$ $\frac{1}{2}$ $\frac{9}{10}$ $1\frac{3}{10}$ $1\frac{3}{5}$

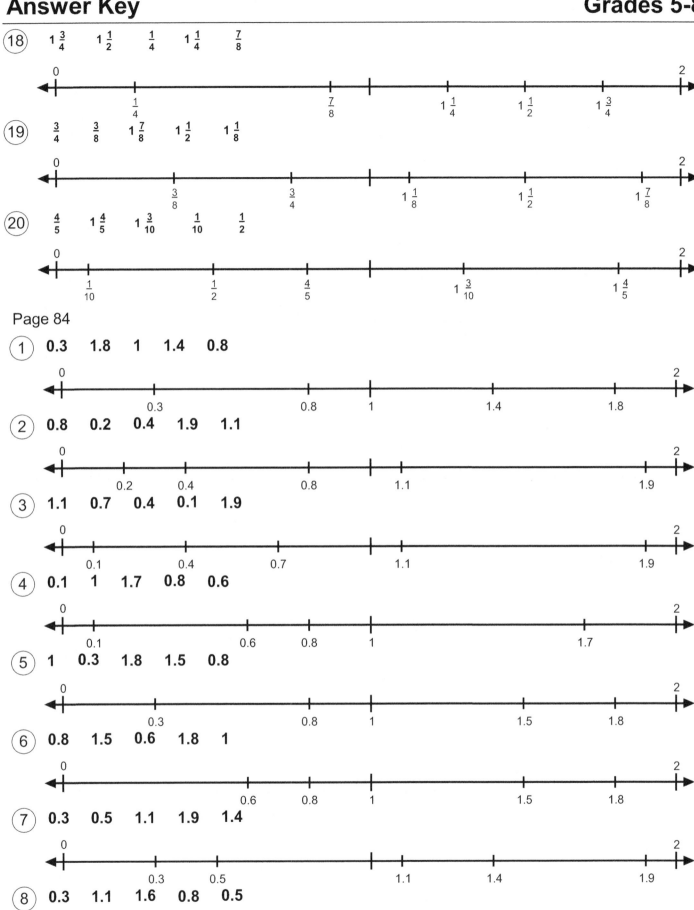

(18) $1\frac{3}{4}$ $1\frac{1}{2}$ $\frac{1}{4}$ $1\frac{1}{4}$ $\frac{7}{8}$

0 ————————————————————————— 2

$\frac{1}{4}$ $\frac{7}{8}$ $1\frac{1}{4}$ $1\frac{1}{2}$ $1\frac{3}{4}$

(19) $\frac{3}{4}$ $\frac{3}{8}$ $1\frac{7}{8}$ $1\frac{1}{2}$ $1\frac{1}{8}$

0 ————————————————————————— 2

$\frac{3}{8}$ $\frac{3}{4}$ $1\frac{1}{8}$ $1\frac{1}{2}$ $1\frac{7}{8}$

(20) $\frac{4}{5}$ $1\frac{4}{5}$ $1\frac{3}{10}$ $\frac{1}{10}$ $\frac{1}{2}$

0 ————————————————————————— 2

$\frac{1}{10}$ $\frac{1}{2}$ $\frac{4}{5}$ $1\frac{3}{10}$ $1\frac{4}{5}$

Page 84

(1) **0.3**   **1.8**   **1**   **1.4**   **0.8**

0 ————————————————————————— 2

0.3   0.8   1   1.4   1.8

(2) **0.8**   **0.2**   **0.4**   **1.9**   **1.1**

0 ————————————————————————— 2

0.2   0.4   0.8   1.1   1.9

(3) **1.1**   **0.7**   **0.4**   **0.1**   **1.9**

0 ————————————————————————— 2

0.1   0.4   0.7   1.1   1.9

(4) **0.1**   **1**   **1.7**   **0.8**   **0.6**

0 ————————————————————————— 2

0.1   0.6   0.8   1   1.7

(5) **1**   **0.3**   **1.8**   **1.5**   **0.8**

0 ————————————————————————— 2

0.3   0.8   1   1.5   1.8

(6) **0.8**   **1.5**   **0.6**   **1.8**   **1**

0 ————————————————————————— 2

0.6   0.8   1   1.5   1.8

(7) **0.3**   **0.5**   **1.1**   **1.9**   **1.4**

0 ————————————————————————— 2

0.3   0.5   1.1   1.4   1.9

(8) **0.3**   **1.1**   **1.6**   **0.8**   **0.5**

0 ————————————————————————— 2

0.3   0.5   0.8   1.1   1.6

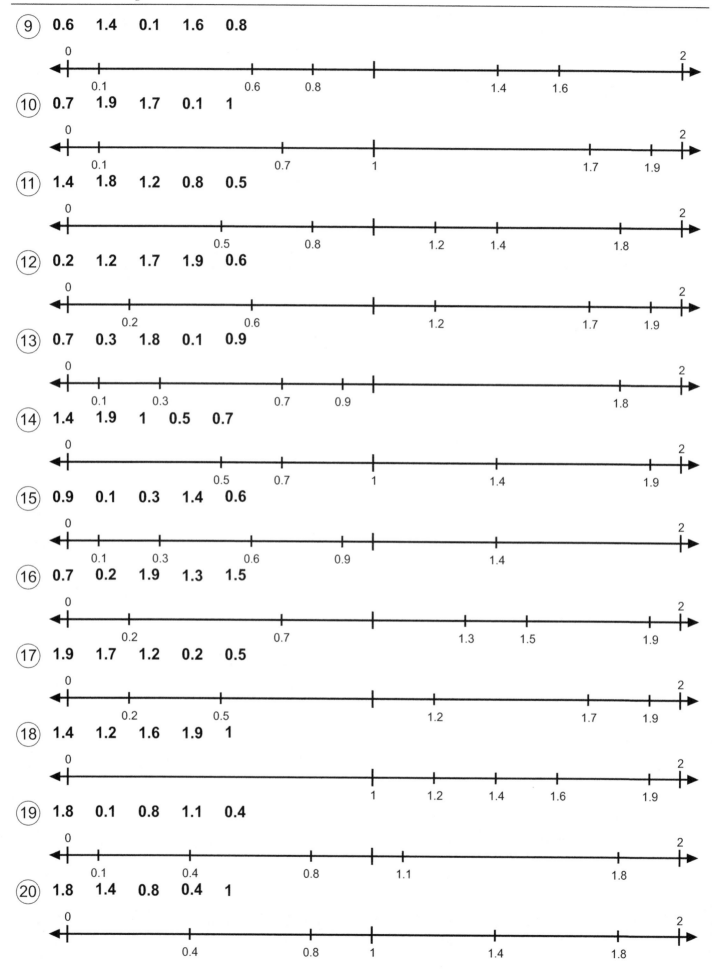

⑨ **0.6 1.4 0.1 1.6 0.8**

⑩ **0.7 1.9 1.7 0.1 1**

⑪ **1.4 1.8 1.2 0.8 0.5**

⑫ **0.2 1.2 1.7 1.9 0.6**

⑬ **0.7 0.3 1.8 0.1 0.9**

⑭ **1.4 1.9 1 0.5 0.7**

⑮ **0.9 0.1 0.3 1.4 0.6**

⑯ **0.7 0.2 1.9 1.3 1.5**

⑰ **1.9 1.7 1.2 0.2 0.5**

⑱ **1.4 1.2 1.6 1.9 1**

⑲ **1.8 0.1 0.8 1.1 0.4**

⑳ **1.8 1.4 0.8 0.4 1**

Printed in Great Britain
by Amazon

47241282R00066